The Glory Man

The Glory Man

A new biography of Billy Bray

by

CYRIL DAVEY

HODDER AND STOUGHTON
LONDON SYDNEY AUCKLAND TORONTO

British Library Cataloguing in Publication Data

Davey, Cyril
   The glory man

   1. Bray, Billy.   2. Evangelists–England–Cornwall–Biography

   1. Title.   269'.2'0924   BV3785.B7

ISBN 0 340 24462 3

First published 1979

Copyright © 1979 by Cyril Davey

Contents

1

Wesley Country

The chapel on the outskirts of the little town was solidly built, Cornish fashion, with blocks of grey granite which would withstand the weather and the years. Rectangular and unadorned it was not a building that seemed to offer much in the way of lightness or excitement. Inside, the pews were brown-stained, and the dominant feature was the pulpit – more a rostrum than a pulpit, indeed, with plenty of room for movement, however unrestrained. It stood facing the congregation, up against the further wall, and below it was a simple table for the celebration of the Lord's Supper.

The crowd inside belied the external impression of solemnity. Anticipation could not be kept within bounds and even whispering produced a surge of sound when the gallery was as full of people as the pews downstairs and the aisles were filled with chairs. One word – one name – obtruded in this busy, eager noise.

'Billy!'

It came again and again, and suddenly there was a turning in the pews, a craning and standing in the gallery to see better as the congregation hushed a little. The preacher, the man who brought out the crowds everywhere, was there. To their excitement Billy Bray added his own as he edged through the crowded aisle towards the pulpit. He did not merely press through them – he skipped and jumped as he moved forward. It was a motion that did not stop when he reached the pulpit. A little man, round-headed and balding, in an old if well-tended black suit, he ran up the steps into the rostrum and – there could be no other word for it – *danced* when he reached it. Even at the beginning of the service his emotion could not be held in check, and it would grow more fervent as he went on.

There would be quips and sallies, leading to explosions of laughter in the plain, godly building. There would be un-ceasing movement as he read or preached. There would be stern accusation, and his invitations to discipleship would be both gentle and gay, loving and authoritative.

Outside the door the waiting stewards had looked at him with concern. A century ago and more there was no public transport in Cornwall, least of all on Sundays, and Billy refused to ride in his horse-trap on that day. To reach this chapel he had walked twenty miles, and he would walk twenty home again.

'Do you want to rest a while before you go in, Mr Bray?' they asked.

'Why should I rest on the Lord's day?'

'Aren't you tired?' one of the men suggested.

Billy laughed out loud. 'All the way here I just put one foot before the other. And every time I put one foot down I shouted "Glory!" and every time I put the other down I cried out "Hallelujah!"'

This was the authentic Billy Bray, the man who could draw crowds – and move them – to the end of his life.

Though he died a century ago he became, and remained, a religious folk-hero of the Methodist people of Cornwall. The simplicity of his faith and the exuberant expression of it kept his name alive long after more immediately influential leaders and more profound thinkers had been forgotten. The only published account of his life – F. W. Bourne's

The King's Son – has continued to sell for a hundred years, yet this man was no more than a simple, self-educated tin-miner ... an eccentric if charismatic lay-preacher ... a 'popular' preacher, certainly, but one who hardly ever crossed the boundary of his own far-western county and then only into the neighbouring towns of Devonshire.

What is there about this emotional – outrageously emotional, some people said – and unsophisticated tin-miner who was 'saved' from drunkenness and degradation, that has caused him to be so well remembered and loved? Not merely his wit and his homely speech, even in the pulpit, though these were passed from mouth to mouth for three generations. The truth seems to be that thousands of conventional and totally-committed Christians wish they had the gaiety and assurance, the uninhibited faith and courage, from which his presentation of the gospel was drawn.

Long dead though he is, an oddity at a time when even in remote west Cornwall worship was becoming more conventional, there is much in the life and character of Billy Bray which can speak to our own materialistic and selfish western society. The word 'western' is not haphazardly used. Much of Asian, and even more of African and Caribbean Christianity, would find this joyous Christian, so uninhibited in the expression of his faith, a man whom they would instantly understand and to whom they would probably instinctively respond. Today, despite our restrained form of worship in the white western world and a comparatively formal church life, there are an increasing number with whom Billy Bray would feel happily at home in his unfettered joy in the Lord.

His story really begins well before his own birth in 1794. It was in the context of Methodism, and especially of its influence on the hard-working and poverty-stricken tin-miners of Cornwall, that his effective and sometimes spectacular lay-ministry became possible. It could have happened at that time in no other church.

Some fifty years before Billy Bray was born, in 1743, a group of horsemen set out from Bristol – a city which had become one of the three main centres of the Methodist revival. London was the city where Wesley had his home (though he spent so much time travelling that he spent comparatively little time there) and it was there that the main institutions of Methodism were established, culminating towards the end of the century in his building of City Road Chapel. Newcastle was the basis of his work in the north, and a convenient staging-post for his travelling preachers. But Bristol, perhaps, was dearest to his heart in the early days. This was the place where he first preached in the open-air, breaking his own formal habit and the accepted rule of the Church of England, of which he was a clergyman. Here he opened the first Methodist preaching-house, built from the contributions of the Methodist people, and still in use for worship. From Bristol some of the earliest Methodist preachers were sent to America, and he established his first school at Kingswood. Five years after Wesley's experience of the 'warmed heart' that was to set England aflame as the revival spread, he set off from Bristol for Cornwall for the first time.

The little party was made up of John Wesley himself, an Anglican clergyman named Shepherd, and two lay-preachers who had already joined the ranks of Wesley's travelling evangelists, John Downes, a well-educated man from the north-east of England, and John Nelson, a stone-mason from Yorkshire. The clergymen had a horse each, but Downes and Nelson shared one between them, taking turns to ride and walk. On the west of England roads, and especially in Cornwall, it was walking-pace for horses as well as foot-travellers. They crossed the Cornish border on Monday, 29th August, and found themselves in what was virtually a foreign country.

Cornwall, like Wales and Scotland, is linked to England by geography but isolated from it by race and tradition. Wales and Cornwall are Celtic in origin, despite a slow admixture of English. In Cornwall there were still people in Wesley's days who spoke the old Cornish language and more who understood it. It was remote in other ways, too, for travel was difficult in England and often almost impossible in parts of Cornwall. The great turnpike roads – the eighteenth-century equivalent of our own motorways – had not been laid down when Wesley went westwards. It was easy to get lost on the great moors and Wesley's party, lost on Bodmin Moor, were only saved long days of wandering in the mist by the sound of Bodmin church-bells. Isolation was not merely a matter of 'miles from London'. The people were inhospitable, and suspicious of strangers whose accents they could not easily comprehend.

Indeed, John Nelson records that on this first visit John Wesley had a wry comment. 'It's a good thing there are plenty of blackberries, brother Nelson, for the people seem to think we can live by preaching!'

But, remote though towns and hamlets were, the news of Wesley's coming was soon generally known. It roused immense interest – no one had ever seen an Anglican parson who rode and preached whenever he wished without seeking permission of the vicar of the parish who might, in any case, have deserted his people more or less permanently for the more sophisticated pleasures of Bath or London. But his preaching also aroused intense opposition, which was sometimes violent, as it was in St Ives. Three weeks after crossing the Cornish border he came to Redruth, the tin-mining capital of Cornwall, and beyond it to Gwennap.

This was the area in which Billy Bray was to grow up and where his family was already living.

The whole countryside, devoid of vegetation except thorny bushes and stunted trees, was scarred and broken up by the tin mines. The bulk of those who lived here gained a precarious living from tin, and almost all of them lived in poverty. Wesley was accustomed to the squalor of the English towns, but here he was thrust into the heart of a country where poverty, illiteracy, appalling living-condit-ions and despondency were almost unrelieved. He knew well enough the sign that hung outside London gin-shops – 'Drunk for a penny, dead-drunk with clean straw to lie on for tuppence'. In the mining-area round Redruth and Truro ale-houses proliferated and offered the same oblivion from the shocking and dangerous work where men hacked out the tin-bearing rock in candle-lit darkness and water-soaked 'levels'.

To such people Wesley was a voice from another world, and he brought a concept of religion alien to anything they had ever imagined. Sin they were accustomed to. It was part of their way of life, and the parish church had little place or significance for them. Religion belonged to the rich, if it had any meaning at all. Salvation was meaningless – until Wesley began to expound it in simple, forthright terms that they could understand.

One of the reasons for Wesley's impact – and, indeed, the effect of Methodism through the century – was that he brought hope to people who had little hope, and the promise of new life to those for whom life was no more than hard labour with an occasional sensual interval, either of sex or drink. No one believed John Wesley would change the con-ditions under which they lived and worked, but many people in that brief visit discovered that the gospel trans-formed life itself. The Cornish are an emotional people, like the Welsh a great singing people, and they responded emotionally to the gospel as it was proclaimed in Methodist terms.

Three-quarters of a century later the excited little miner, Billy Bray, was to have the same effect, though in a much more limited fashion and in somewhat changed conditions.

On that first visit Wesley stayed in the little mining village of Carharrack and, when he wakened between three and four in the morning, it was to the sound of singing. Outside was an excited crowd of 'tinners' who wanted to be sure of hearing him preach and were passing the hours of waiting in the darkness 'in singing and praising God'. In so short a time, less than a month after he had arrived in the county, the transformation of the mining community had begun.

True, there was opposition. In Cornwall, as in the rest of England, the well-bred and affluent society – Wesley's caustic word for them was 'respectable' – reacted strongly against him and against his converts. It would be absurd to suggest that every tin-miner became a Methodist or a Christian – most did not. But the Carharrack miners were evidence of an early awakening to the gospel and as he preached there were emotional – some would say hysterical – scenes as people cried out from conviction and spiritual release, from anguish over the past and joy over sins forgiven. It was an apparently unlikely result of preaching, itself unemotional, by a highly-educated and self-contained Anglican clergyman. There is nothing that can explain it except the powerful moving of the spirit of God, as Wesley 'offered Christ' – in his own much-used phrase.

Not far from Carharrack, where he was staying, was a place to become famous in the Methodist story, which would remain a place of pilgrimage to our own time. This was Gwennap Pit.

A series of old 'mine-workings' had collapsed and the earth above had caved in, leaving a rough, rocky, natural amphitheatre that made an ideal site for a preacher in the open air. Some three hundred feet wide and four hundred feet long, it was about fifty feet deep, and thousands of people could find a place in it, while the flat ground around it could accommodate as many as cared to gather there. Because of its natural acoustics Wesley, who despite his small stature had a clear, precise and commanding voice, regarded it as one of the easiest places he ever had to speak in. It was to be a regular stopping-place on the thirty-two preaching tours he made of Cornwall until his death in 1791.

On this first visit, when someone told of the old mine-workings, he took his crowd with him and it swelled on the way. Thousands of people sat quietly while he spoke. His text was: 'Believe on the Lord Jesus Christ and thou shalt be saved.' There were many who did so, while others confirmed their newly-found experience of grace.

Amongst those who were part of the listening crowds on occasion – which grew, so Wesley said, to twenty-five thousand by the time of his last visit – was a tin-miner named Bray. Where he heard Welsey preach first we do not know, but he certainly became one of his most devoted followers in the Redruth area and his home was only a mile or so away from Busveal where the 'Pit' was situated.

Bray's home was at Twelveheads, some five or six miles from Redruth and a couple of miles from Carharrack where Wesley was wakened by the singing miners. This whole area was dominated by engine-houses at the headworks of the mines. The landscape was bare and treeless with little more than a sparse covering of reddish earth over the granite rock. Mine shafts and adits, black holes dug into the earth, pock-marked the ground and, below the surface, the earth was honey-combed with the narrow tunnels in which the miners worked. A low hill, Carn Marth, rocky and gorse-covered, was the only break in the level surroundings and from its summit could be seen mile after mile of country scarred and broken by the mining operations. Ting Tang, Wheal Moyle and Wheal Squire lay at the foot of the hill ('wheal' is old Cornish for 'mine'); St Day United Mines with Creegbrawse and Penkival were a little further away; the Great Consolidated Mines, with ten engine houses to United's seven, sprawled over the countryside together with Clifford Mines, East Falmouth, Baddern and Wheal Jane. It is easy to see why John Wesley, who always preferred industrial missioning to rural rides, found himself at home in west Cornwall. In those days it was one of the busiest parts of industrial Britain.

The tin-miners who worked the mines had few amenities except the ale-houses, though they occasionally earned good money if a mine was prosperous. Their homes were no better than hovels, and Twelveheads was typical of the worst of these scattered hamlets. There were a few thatched dwellings, single-storey cottages made of 'cob' – earth, mud and straw bound together – containing a couple of tiny rooms, an open hearth, apertures for windows shrouded with a bit of sacking (the tax on glass made glazing impossible for any but the better-off), and a floor of hard-beaten earth. The more respectable were clean, many of the rest filthy. Nearby was a patch of scrubby land, dominated by granite outcrops, in which the poor grew potatoes. Working conditions were inhuman, poverty was endemic and universal, and the further edge of starvation was all too familiar to families whose men stopped at the ale-house on their way home from work – and often never even reached home before their next 'turn' came to go down the mine.

Miner Bray quickly showed the practical results of 'conversion' after he had responded to Wesley's preaching. His home became cleaner, the potatoes were tended more carefully to provide more food, and the atmosphere in which his family grew up was wholesomely cleared of oaths, quarrels, bawdy songs and the stench of poor ale. In their place came careful accounting, a sense of love and the three constant punctuations of Methodist household life – Bible-reading, prayers and hymn-singing. It was very easy to see, in Twelveheads or any other village, which homes had been changed by the Methodist revival. And what many critics regarded as rigid and unrelieved godliness the Brays, and those like them, found to be the source of peace and continuing joy.

The children of such a household were likely to be won to the same experience because they had known both 'before' and 'after'. They knew what conversion meant because they shared gratefully in the results of it. For the next generation, however, the 'holy discipline' of Bible-reading before breakfast and after a meagre supper, followed by prayers in which the same phrases obtruded day by day, was not always so exciting! There were those who rebelled inwardly if not outwardly, and the rebellion was strengthened by the taunts of friends who grew up in very different households.

One of those who rebelled was miner Bray's grandson, Billy.

Bray brought up his children to his own pattern and they shared his own Christian faith and experience. His son continued in his father's way when he married and his own family were expected to reproduce the same effects. Of this marriage there were at least four children, including two boys, James and Billy – who was born in 1794 – and two girls, one of whom was apparently mentally disturbed.

Unhappily the father died young and, though their mother survived for many years until, in old age, she became blind as well as feeble, the children did not remain with her but were taken over by their grandfather and grandmother.

Young Billy Bray was extrovert, talkative, popular and ready to show off on any occasion. He disliked discipline and had a strong character of his own. In a religious society where all the commandments seemed to begin with 'thou shalt not' he was not an easy or a likely subject for the typical Methodist conversion which his father and grandfather had known, or for the quiet, regulated life which they had led.

Rebellion, rather than religion, was life to young Billy. And that was the path he would follow, when the time came – almost to disaster.

2

Escape to Devon

'I went to Devon, to work in the mines there,' says Billy Bray in his journal. It is an ill-written account of his life and experiences, with poor spelling and crabbed writing, often hard to follow, but despite its illiteracy it is the nearest we come to the man himself, and some of its phrases are crisp indeed.

'When I was there I lived a bad life . . .'

'During that time I was very near hell.'

This was no casual, throw-away phrase. As we follow him across the Devon border and back to Twelveheads at the end of seven years of hard labour, rough living, sin and inner anguish, it is an exact statement of the truth as he knew it. Even when he returned to Twelveheads he was on the brink of hell, and sunk deep in it in his own mind for another five years.

What caused him to go to Devon, or made this young man of seventeen who had been brought up in the devoutest of families rebel as he did? The truth is fairly clear – it was *too* devout for a youth who was by temperament vigorous, extrovert and individualistic, who always found it hard to keep his mouth closed, and whose unconventional nature was alienated by the conventional respectability of 'chapel life'.

Billy's grandfather was a staunch Methodist who had

heard John Wesley preach, been converted during one of his visits, and had found his life turned into a new mould. The result was joy and freedom in his heart, a new power in his life and a determination to bring up his family in ways which would enable them to share his own experience. Not only so, but he wished to share what he had with others. There was no place in which his fellow-Methodists could gather at Twelveheads except the small rooms of their own cottages and so Grandfather Bray, beginning what was to be triplicated in his grandson's own life, built a small chapel for the Methodists to worship in. Billy never seems to have criticised his grandfather publicly – and his grandfather was the centre of the household, for he can hardly have known his father well before he died and the children moved to Grandfather Bray's house – but he must certainly have resented the rigidity of Methodist behaviour.

'A bunch of old hypocrites' was his own description of Methodists, and that he had to conform, at least outwardly, to his grandfather's views produced the tensions in his nature that eventually exploded into rebellion.

The focal points of Methodist life were public worship in the chapel, simpler worship at home, and the 'class-meeting'. For the most part Sunday worship was conducted by lay-preachers; there were far too many chapels for the circuit minister to be appointed to any of the smaller ones very often. The lay preachers were well known, and the content of their message familiar. Often it was condemnatory, and both sin and damnation were the subject-matter, added to the plain exposition of a Bible story. The 'characters' amongst them were rare, though they certainly existed – and this was one reason why Billy Bray, a few years later, was to become so well-known a preacher and personality. The small chapels seem to have been reasonably well-filled, but those who came expected little out of the ordinary and seldom found it.

The 'class-meeting' was peculiarly a Methodist institution for, from the very early days, Wesley had gathered his people in each 'society' into small groups of a dozen people with a lay leader. In theory every member was expected to attend 'class' every week and to speak openly of his experience – his sins and failures, his triumphs and spiritual victories and, above all, his *present* experience of the grace of God. In practice, what had begun as a joy became for many people at the best a weekly ritual and at the worst a reluctant chore. The 'temptations' and 'triumphs' were as familiar as those who spoke of them and, all too often, the same 'experience' was recounted week after week, or even month after month. There was reality in it, but little growth in grace or knowledge. The result was that some people stayed away because they had nothing to say, and others because they had heard all that their neighbours had to say too many times before.

The class-meeting, too, was to find itself transformed when Billy eventually had an experience to speak about. That experience was to be living, renewed and recounted with a verve and enthusiasm that was often astonishing.

The expression of the Methodist faith was ideally in personal witness, prayer, Bible-reading, conversation and, most notably, hymn-singing. Anyone who attended worship regularly, as Billy certainly had to do for most of his youth, knew the most familiar Bible-passages off by heart – but he knew the hymns off by heart, too. And in Methodism both theology and Bible were reproduced in the hymns that were sung. Unfortunately, if the tunes were vigorous enough, they could be sung – with the Cornishman's natural talent for part-singing – loudly enough to shake the rafters without anyone taking much notice of the words, the theology they expounded or the spiritual experience they enshrined.

The thought of Billy one day down the mine, walking the roads or on his way to a preaching appointment singing because he meant every word would have seemed impossible to those who watched him fidgeting in his grandfather's pew in the Twelveheads chapel!

As to 'good conversation' and personal witness Billy would have said – and often did say – that he had had enough of it to last his lifetime. For 'Christian converse' all too frequently consisted of talk about other people that was little better than mere gossip, salted with a self-righteous condemnation of them for their sinful ways. At the same time, as Billy himself said many times later, 'witness' was almost non-existent where it was needed most.

'There were plenty of Christians down the mine when I was a bad man, joking and jeering about religion, but none who ever reproved me for my words or spoke to me of Christ!'

It may be that they would have received a witty, wicked and devastating reply if they had done, but for Billy the truth remained that 'personal witness' was all too often lacking amongst those who were quickest to condemn in the safety of a class-meeting or a pulpit.

It is not, perhaps, difficult to see why he gibed at them as hypocrites – though there is nothing to suggest that he ever included his grandfather in his vicious sneers.

There was nothing at all to produce joy, originality or even the hope of heaven except as an eventual escape, in the tin-mining scene round Twelveheads where Billy lived the first seventeen years of his life. On the other hand, there was plenty that seemed both hopeless and hellish.

An elegant young man who visited the area, presumably from the sophisticated delights of London's society, in the year before Billy Bray was born was horrified by what he saw.

'I found a bleak desert, made more doleful by the un-healthy appearance of the inhabitants. At every step ladders go down into utter darkness or funnels exhale warm copper-ous vapours. All around the openings tin and copper ore is piled in heaps waiting for purchasers. This ore is drawn hot and reeking out of the mines by 'whims" put in motion by donkeys which are driven round the circles by devilish children hanging over the poor brutes and flogging them round without respite.

'This scene continues for miles. Everywhere there are huge iron engines, creaking and groaning. Tall chimneys stand by them, smoking and flaming. The whole place is reminiscent of hell.

'I saw several woeful figures in tattered garments, with pick-axes on their shoulders, crawl out of a dark fissure in the ground and repair to a hovel near the entrance to this crack in the ground. This is the gin-shop and here for the few hours allotted to them above ground they seek oblivion.'

Had this young London visitor followed them beyond the gin-shop to their own homes he would have found them hovels, too. And if he had had the temerity to follow them back down the hole in the ground he would have understood why they looked woeful and their appearance was miserable and unhealthy.

Young Billy may well have been one of the boys who, at some mine-shaft or another, drove the donkeys endlessly round to winch the ore from the depths below. Certainly he would have gone to work in the narrow tunnels below ground as soon as he could carry tools or wield a pick. There was nothing else to do in Twelveheads. There was no schooling in these hamlets for poor miners' children. If a child learned to read, or to write intelligibly, he did so at home from a father or more likely a mother who had had the good fortune of a little education from their own parents. Because of their wide use of hymns and the Bible this was more likely to be the case in Methodist homes than most others.

Work stopped in the mines on Sundays, except for urgent

matters. It was a day for rest, parish worship, or chapel-going. For the common 'tinners' it would almost certainly be 'chapel' or nothing. The parish churches were still, almost everywhere, the reserve of the wealthy, the respectable, the ambitious and their retainers, with a formal reading of the prayer-book and a brief homily, quickly read and unheeded. The exhausting work underground for six days of the week made one day's rest essential.

Below ground Billy was in a dark world, lit by candles. There was the sound and flow of running water, the crash of pick and shovel reverberating in the narrow tunnels, the occasional creaking of the rock itself which made every miner stop work to see if it heralded the real danger of a 'fall', and the throaty sound of men's voices, swearing, talking or even singing. Billy found the talk very different from his grandfather's house, and increasingly he began to join in it. The jokes were usually bawdy and the conversation often salacious, and as he grew older Billy gained a reputation for wit. He was quickly recognised as a mocker and a mimic, and his companions encouraged him in it because it belied his heritage and his Methodist background. No one could make more bitter mockery of chapel and preachers than this youth who was condemned to sit there Sunday by Sunday, whether he wished it or not.

But, however he behaved below ground, there was one place forbidden him once he was on the surface. That was the 'kiddleywink', the Cornish miners' name for the gin-shop at the shaft-top. He saw men go in hungrily, for they often sold food as well as drink, and saw them come out reeling drunk. One day, swore young Billy, he would get as drunk as they were and no one should stop him. He heard the fiddler scraping away and promised himself to join in the bawdy singing – and lead it, too, once he had escaped from his grandfather's eye. He looked at the miner's women, in their tawdry finery, and lusted for someone like them.

One day. ....

At the age of seventeen he could stand home and chapel and the bursting tension in himself no longer. Miners went from Cornwall over the border to find work in the Devon mines. Some of his own friends were there already. He would escape, whatever his family said.

And break away he did.

He could never forget those years in Devon, where he sank lower and lower into degradation and, in his unoccupied and sober moments, into self-disgust. He would, indeed, spend most of his life paying back to God the debt he owed for forgiveness of them, and wiping out their misery with a joyous proclamation of the gospel of grace. But, while they lasted, the seven years were misery in spite of all the pranks and drinking, the work and whoring that he put into them.

The mines of South Devon were little different from those in Cornwall, but for Billy the change lay in his ability to choose his own company, spend his money as he liked and do what he wished. Very quickly he began to drink, and bad ale and gin rotted his system, corroded his temper and affected his work. He was disciplined by the mine 'captain' and, when he argued with him and lost his temper, he lost his job as well. But there were other mines, and other jobs. He moved to Tavistock, and took lodgings in, of all places, a beer shop.

Sober, he was an amusing companion, a witty man full of fun, quick repartee, racy speech and laughter. Drunk, he was argumentative, bad-tempered and violent, though there was nothing unusual in his pranks or his behaviour. One night, staggering home drunk with his friends, they found a cart-horse and climbed onto its back to ride it to their lodgings. Instead, when it stumbled over a stone in the dark, they rolled off its back and thought themselves lucky not to have been killed or kicked to death. Again, one of his

23

brawls turned into an open fight and his miner's hat fell into the fire and was burned. He stole another and barely escaped being gaoled for it. But fighting was the inevitable result of drinking, and the edge rubbed off life as the years went by. If he was still full of fun he was equally prone to what he called 'mad frolics'. The rebellious youth became a wild and undisciplined man. There were cheap women in the beer-houses of Devon, as there were in Cornwall, and his old lust revived – but that led to fights, too. Even worse for Billy, it led to a bad conscience which had to be stifled, if it could, by heavier drinking. It was not a period for correspond-ence and Billy would have had little written communication with his own home, but news travelled by word of mouth as miners moved between Cornwall and Devon. Twelveheads was not so far away, after all, and he could not wholly escape the memory of family and home, drown it as he would. Certainly 'chapel' had no place in his week's activities. When work stopped on Saturday his place was in the beer-house not the pew.

There were moments when his physical safety was threatened more dreadfully than in his drunken fights. One stayed vividly in his memory throughout his life. 'I was working underground,' he said, 'when I heard a "scat" (a breaking of the rock) over my head. I ran out and I think forty tons of it fell down where I had been working a mo-ment before.'

Billy was discovering that though he could run away, there was no escape. He could not run away from himself, or from the God whom he had heard preached about so often. The conflict within himself grew more terrible to bear.

In the beer-shop, with other drunkards, 'I drank all night long. But I had a sore head and a sick stomach, and worse, than all, horrors of mind that no tongue can tell. I used to dread to go to sleep for fear of waking up in hell. And, though I made many promises to the Lord to be better, I was soon as bad or worse than ever.'

The years dragged by, and Billy's divided mind meant that he was never at peace. He was torn apart by fear and contrition, by the occasional aching desire to reform and the impossibility of doing so. He was haunted by dreams of hell and saw no way of drawing away from the edge of it.

He had run away to Devon to escape the rigid demands of a chapel-going society. Perhaps, he thought increasingly often, he could run away to Cornwall once more to escape the clutches of the devil who had such a terrifyingly firm hold of him in Devon.

At the end of seven years of moving from mine to mine, village to village, ale-house to ale-house and sin to worse sin, he made up his mind.

He would go home. And so, indeed, he did. At the age of twenty-four, a hardened man instead of a venturesome youth, he returned to Cornwall. His own succinct account of it is sombre and without hope.

'I came home a drunkard.'

3

The Years of Tension

His return to Cornwall was the beginning of another five years of increasing mental anguish, a period in which he alternated between a sottish addiction to drink and a silent longing to be free of it. This deeply divided state of mind seems to have been hidden from and unrecognised by all who knew him. It was a time of agony which he suffered alone. To have admitted it would have put him at the mercy of the mockers – the men who looked at him as leader in their condemnation of religion and scorn for all who professed to be Christians.

How his family reacted to his home-coming Billy does not record in his journal, but their relief at having him back must have very quickly turned to humiliation at what he had become. His fellow-miners, on the other hand, must have found almost endless amusement in his descriptions of life in Devon. He was a born raconteur, and nothing would have been lost in his telling of tale after tale. The fall from the horse, the women he had known and conquered or bought, the stolen hat, the smart answers he had given to mine-captains and overseers, his mimicry of travelling preachers ... to a man with a quick wit, a fluent use of words and an ability to come to terms with his listeners and win them to his side, these and innumerable other unrecorded happenings made him the centre of any group of tinners, below or above ground. Of his inner state he said nothing, covering his unease with a veneer of salty conversation and irreligious quips.

He would have had little difficulty in getting work once he was back in Twelveheads. If mines closed others quickly opened, and there is some evidence that he was a skilful worker.

But what was the work of a 'tinner' when Billy came back to Cornwall? In following the story of his exuberant life it is important to remember the background of hardship, rough labouring conditions and uncertainty which were always part of it. Except for fishing round the coasts, with a dash of smuggling thrown in, and the unrewarding cultivation of a small-holding or croft (usually as a secondary occupation), there was very little work in West Cornwall apart from the mines. And most men, when they went down the mine for the first time, knew that it was an occupation which would leave them stunted in body and shorten their lives.

All the Cornish mines depended on 'mining adventurers'. They might be local men – landed gentry, land-owning farmers, businessmen with offices in Truro or Falmouth – working on their own with borrowed capital from the private banks in the bigger Cornish towns, or a consortium of 'foreigners' from England who hoped for a quick return on a chancy investment. Those who have read Winston Graham's 'Poldark' books or seen the television series will have some idea of the uncertainties the 'adventurers' faced. Both tin and copper were the metals they sought, and there was plenty below the granite outcrops which covered the Cornish landscape. But 'prospecting' with no scientific equipment depended on little more than chance – the finding of ore at a hitherto unsuspected outcrop of rocks, the gossip passed from mouth to mouth and father to son about the way some copper or tin lode ran in a disused mine, or even the shrewd salesmanship of a glib-tongued 'con-man'.

The investor stood to lose a great deal of money expended

in sinking shafts, employing workers and extracting the ore – and if the first few attempts failed he might well give up when a further sinking of the shaft would have filled his pockets. On the other hand, a shrewd knowledge of local conditions and mineralogy, matched by money and perseverance, could make him a fortune. It would never do that for the men employed below ground, though from time to time they might make good money for a period.

The miner often did not even know who owned the mine where he worked, and certainly would seldom see them, even if they were local magnates. The key-figure was the 'purser', the administrator who controlled the whole enterprise and provided shareholders with regular accounts, often in monthly shareholders' meetings, which showed whether it was worth the continuing risk of their money, or not. At the mine itself it was the 'captain' who held the real responsibility – and the title continued to exist in tin-mining and smelting almost to the present day. He supervised everything, delegated authority below ground to sub-captains, and looked for men who could be trusted to exercise it. Between the 'captain' and the miners was an immense gulf. The same young man who described the mining scene in the St Day area, quoted in the last chapter, went on to make a note about the managers.

'I saw two strange Cornish beings in long white duck-coats. This was the uniform of the "captains". They inhabit tolerable houses where the mine inspectors, who come on behalf of the owners, regale them upon beef, pudding and brandy.' A notable contrast to the 'woeful figures' who trudged off to the ale-house!

There would be days in the future when Billy himself would be employed in the responsible tasks of a 'sub-captain' in one or other small mine, but it was not something he could look forward to when he joined his old acquaintances at the head of the shaft at Twelveheads.

The shaft itself was a wide, deep hole plunging into the

darkness below. When Billy's grandfather began work the shafts could be no deeper than some ninety fathoms at the most. By the time Billy came back from Devon the great mining engineers, Boulton and Watt, and Trevithick, had made it possible to sink shafts to 200 fathoms, that is 1,200 feet. The invention that made this possible was the new pumping-engine. There seemed to be water just below the surface in many mines, and at 90 fathoms the 'levels' were so flooded that men had to work up to their knees or even their waists in water reddened by copper ore. The new engines effectively pumped the water and cleared the levels for another 600 feet.

The descent was terrifying, and required a great deal of courage and exemplary care. The wall of the shaft was the natural rock and earth through which the diggers had hewed a way downwards. Against the shaft-wall were long ladders, the end of the first attached to the top of the second, and so on down the whole depth of the mine. These ladders were movable, and were linked with a donkey-engine accommodated in the tall engine-houses which now add such a romantic touch to the Cornish landscape. As the engine worked the ladders moved up and down the shaft. Billy and his fellows moved out over the open space of the pit, clambered onto the ladder and climbed downwards. At the bottom of the ladder they stepped onto a small platform built into the side of the shaft. The engine roared, the ladder jerked upwards and the ladder below came to rest by the platform. The miner swung back onto it and was jerked downwards again – deeper and deeper while the opening to the sky seemed to grow smaller and smaller until it was a mere star of light hundreds of feet above his head. His only illumination was a candle stuck into his hat – and, as Billy knew from his Devonshire frolics, for a miner to lose his hat was to lose his livelihood until he could get a new one. From the platforms low tunnels – 'levels', in the miners' speech – ran outwards into the rock, with candles stuck at intervals along the 'walls'. When he had reached the level at which he was working the miner passed along it, often almost doubled up, to take up the task of hewing out the rock where he had left off at the end of the last 'core' or shift.

It was a dangerous life indeed. A hand slipping on the ladder as it went up or down, a false step on or off the small platform at the side of the shaft, would inevitably mean plunging to death at the bottom of the shaft. And, every year, there were many men who did so. Billy knew well enough from experience that the surest way to certain death was to go carelessly from the ale-house to the shaft. An unsteady hand, a fuddled eye that misjudged distance, might herald the awful scream of terror he had heard too often as men plunged downwards. But, back in the St Day and Twelveheads mines, it was not merely the death-fall that Billy dreaded. For him, he believed emphatically, the mine-shaft would in those circumstances be the entrance to hell itself.

It is not surprising that hell had so strong a hold on his imagination.

Few people today would think that the risk was worth the cost of the candles! Then, it was the mines, with all the risk involved, or starvation. When the 'captain' had decided whether new shafts were to be sunk, new 'levels' made or old ones extended, the number of 'pitches' to be worked and the number of men needed to work them, he called a 'Setting Day'. At this the pitches – the working-places in the levels – were auctioned off to the lowest bidder. That is to say, the man who got the 'pitch' was the man who was willing to work it for least money. But this was never an individual bid or task, for the pitches were worked by teams of anything from two to eight men. For the most part, by Billy's records, he worked in small groups, The workers were charged for tools, candles, blasting powder, and the cost of hauling the rock or ore they cut to the surface where it was processed. The account was settled at the next 'setting day', usually held every month. A hard-working team in a good seam where the ore was rich could earn good money. The opposite was equally true.

This, then, was the background to the whole of Billy's working life. It was a frightening existence below ground as well as a desperately arduous one. The Cornish miners were intensely superstitious and the darkness was full of fears. Every miner knew the 'knackers' – the hidden men who hammered on the walls beyond where they themselves were working at their own unseen and untapped levels. Cornishmen believed that these were the spirits of Jews who lived in the days of Christ, jeered at his crucifixion and had been condemned to work in the Cornish mines until doomsday. But if the long-held tradition was nonsense the sound of the knackers was an intimation of danger and many miners would desert their own pitch rather than stay and wait to see what happened. Most miners had their own stories of hearing the knackers and getting out of the level only just in time to escape a rock-fall from the roof. 'Knackers' or not, roof and rock falls were real and men died from them as certainly as from slipping off a ladder and falling down the shaft.

That Billy was neither seriously injured underground nor fell to his death down the shaft after some drunken spree his companions could only put down to the worst of reasons.

'Old Billy has the luck of the devil hisself!'

'Ess – the devil looks after his own!'

The comments were typical and more than half-believed. If Billy had a recurring feeling that 'God was giving him another chance' he only half-believed that, too, and turned his back both on God and on each additional opportunity for repentance.

A year or two after he came back from Devon he married.

To the end of his life he referred to his wife only as 'Joey', and there is little in Billy's record about how he met her or why they married. Probably he did not 'meet' her at all. The mining villages of the St Day area were close together, with much intermarriage, and the movement of men from mine to mine, as one opened or another closed, meant that few people were strangers to each other. Marriage was the normal state of a man as he grew older, and a common prelude to it in many rural parts of Britain was pregnancy. Girls married because they 'had to' if they were to remain respectable. Love there must have been in many marriages, but both men and women knew each too well to have any illusions about their partner or their future.

Joey could have had no illusions whatever about Billy. She herself had been a 'chapel girl' and passed through the usual phase of 'responding to an appeal' as a prelude to being recognised as a member of the Methodist 'society'. Billy's journal has a brief reference to the fact that Joey had been converted but had 'gone back' before her marriage. Certainly when the time came she was able to speak with longing of a lost experience of peace and joy.

There was, however, neither peace nor joy for the young bride in being Billy's wife, and she probably expected none. He was, as they said, 'not much to look at'. Like most Celts and almost all Cornish miners, he was short, spare and wiry. His clothes were shabby and tattered. But it may well be that his eyes were irresistible, for when he was sober they danced with fun and his plain face lit up with merriment. He was good company, too – witty and caustic, even if he was coarse with it. To his friends he was the best company they knew, for with them he let himself go completely. 'I was the wildest, most daring and reckless of all the reckless, daring men. I was the worst of the lot.'

As a miner's daughter Joey had known what it was to go short of necessities, but married to Billy she was faced with much worse hardship and humiliation. The beer-shop was inevitably the cause of it. Billy looked back later with pity for what she had to suffer.

'At one time I had good money for two months successively, but £5 of it went on drink. I sinned against light and knowledge.'

'At another time I remember I went to get some coal. There was a beer-shop in the way and coming home I went in. My poor wife was forced to come for me and wheel home the coal herself. A drunkard would rather spend his money on drink than give it to his wife and children.'

Joey must have given up hope as she had given up religion. And yet, perhaps, not entirely. Whatever anyone else knew, she suspected the turmoil that went on in her husband's nature. Billy, like all drunkards, was maudlin when he rolled home from mine and kiddleywink. The old tug-of-war that had begun within himself in Devon was becoming more evident. He would drink himself sick, and moan about his folly. 'I never got drunk without being condemned for it', he wrote. If his conscience tormented him by day, this was nothing compared to the horror of his dreams at night. Hell was a recurrent nightmare, and Joey, listening to his outbursts as he rolled in terror by her side, could do little to soothe him. Someone who had fallen from grace seemed a poor support for a man who had never known it – and yet Billy longed for comfort. His inner agony was increasingly insupportable. If there were many times when he narrowly escaped falling down one of the innumerable unfenced, disused mine-shafts, there were others when he wished that he had done so. Indeed, there were not a few nights when he contemplated going out of his hovel-like cottage and jumping down a shaft to end it all.

Not that his companions in the mine realised what he was feeling. Indeed, the stronger the night-time determination to change his ways became, the more violent were his outbursts against God and religion. There was a time which he never forgot when his irreligious cronies stood back in horror. 'So fearful was his blasphemy that they declared his oaths must come from Hell itself.'

'You smell of sulphur, Billy!' said one of them, staring at him.

But the tension was moving towards crisis point.

4

Crisis

In the Greek of the New Testament the word *krisis* means 'judgment', and we have simply taken the word over into our English vocabulary. With us, it means a moment of danger, suspense, possibly the beginning of disaster. In medical terms it is 'the turning point', for better or worse. To use the word of those seven days in November, 1823, when Billy worked down the tin-mine haunted by John Bunyan's visions ... when he went into the ale-house and could not drink ... when he came home and agonised with his wife or rolled in anguish in and out of bed is to give it its fullest possible meaning. This was 'crisis' indeed. Billy was horribly aware of judgment, saw himself in deepest danger, knew the awful suspense that he might never escape from it. It was, in spiritual terms, the 'turning point'.

For a few days he thought he might not survive it.

John Wesley had insisted that his Methodist community should be a 'reading people'. He published a 'Christian Library' of religious and other classics. But, in the main, his people could not afford books with the exception of the Bible and his own published hymn-books which, in the early days, all the various divisions of Methodism still used. The Cornish miners had little use or time for education, and even their children were expected to work as soon as they could walk. The money the children earned was little enough, but it was an extra pittance which stood between the family and starvation. Not until the 1870s was a notice placarded in the Redruth streets insisting that children of nine years old must have two hours of schooling a day, however long they worked in the mine. Most Methodist children, however, learned to read at home and at worship. Their educational diet was the Bible and the hymn-book. And for many of them the lines they learned they never completely forgot.

If Billy had not been a Methodist, and thus able to read (however ill he scrawled and spelt) he would not have picked up the one book which came into his hands at this point and changed his life. This was John Bunyan's *Visions of Heaven and Hell*. It shows something of his turmoil of spirit that he began to read it as soon as he got hold of it, starting with the visions of heaven. But 'heaven' was far beyond his hopes and he found himself gripped most horribly, instead, by the 'visions of hell'.

It was in the middle of that week that he went to work, joining his 'core' (the little group of men who had paid for the privilege of working one pitch of rock) down the mine. His close friend, Sam Coad, was well aware of his misery though perhaps only suspecting the cause of it and set out to jolly him out of his gloom. Billy's responses were half-hearted. In the forefront of his mind was one of Bunyan's appalling pictures – two friends in hell, tormenting each other though they loved each other in life.

He muttered to himself, though his friend did not catch the phrase. 'Shall Sam Coad and I torment each other in hell?'

The shift over he trudged home, wet with mine-water, reddened by the tin and copper ore, as shabby in his thoughts as he looked in his thin, bedraggled clothes.

Joey gazed at him in pain of heart, perplexed about how to help him. 'You should seek the Lord, Billy,' she said. Looking back on her own experience, now lost to her, she went on. 'No tongue can tell what they enjoy who serve the Lord!'

He looked round the shabby kitchen, at his wife with her torn dress and the children in rags. There was no joy there. 'Then why don't you begin again?' She stared at him, with no answer. 'If you did, then I might begin, too!' She still had no answer and he went on, half-angrily. 'Show me how to be saved. You're much less of a sinner than I am. You'd soon be forgiven and you can get me converted, too.'

But it was no use. She was as lost as himself and he went to bed tortured and disconsolate. Should he get down on his knees and pray? What would Joey say? Would she laugh at him? Tell him he was beyond hope? He climbed into bed, under the worn sheeting, and tried to sleep. At three o'clock he crawled out again, escaping from the Bunyan-stimulated nightmares. Without a look at the sleeping Joey, he fell on his knees and began to pray. It was the first time he had knelt to pray since he was a boy – and probably the first time in his life he had truly poured his whole being into his prayer. How long he prayed he never recorded or spoke about. It may well have seemed either like a minute or so, or like an age. But when he rose from his knees he was a changed man.

The change in him – and it was evident enough to his fellow-miners the next day – was not a dramatic, sudden and momentary conversion, a swift flash of light from heaven that brought him blinded to his knees. He was to spend hours on his knees before certainty eventually came. Indeed, almost a week would pass before he could say, as he did, 'I am a new man altogether.' In some ways it must have seemed like the typical, traditional Methodist conversion experience – at least to those who worked with him or saw him every week in the ale-house. But Joey, who had seen him wrestling with fear and guilt, knew that the struggle had gone on for months. His resistance to grace and love, matched by ever wilder and more blasphemous language and behaviour, was such as led many of the Methodists in the previous century to the cries of anguish, followed by an exhausted coma, which Welsey and others describe frequently enough. But, for Billy, release did not come in that traumatic fashion. He had begun to pray and had begun to change, but the long years of turmoil which had started when he was in Devon years earlier were not to be resolved in an instantaneous conversion. He was to pray his way into peace for days. Yet that peace was to be the harbinger of a joy which, for the rest of his life, he could hardly contain.

Friday was 'setting day' or pay-day and the miners moved from the mine-head almost, it seemed, involuntarily to the ale-houses to spend what they had earned. Billy had been quiet enough as he chipped away at the granite rock below ground – so quiet, indeed, that his friends thought he must be ill. Their suspicions were confirmed when he got to the ale-house.

'Nothin' to drink for me!' said Billy.

'Sick in the stomach are 'ee, boy?' asked one.

'No,' he answered. 'I don't feel like it.' It was as far as he would commit himself, but he did not leave.

The talk, more bawdy as the ale flowed, rattled round the crowded room, filled mainly with men while a few women, blowsy and pock-marked, cackled with tipsy laughter on the narrow bench by the door.

'You look sour as a preacher,' grinned one of his workmates, and slapped him on his thin shoulders with an oath.

Billy rounded on him. 'You'll give an account for words like that one day.'

The talk fell away round them. 'What's the matter with 'ee, Billy? Do 'ee want us all to go up the class-meeting at the chapel or something?'

There was a shout of laughter, and the tinners, their clothes still damp with mine-water and steaming in the heat of the room, waited for Billy to respond with one of his viciously amusing quips about the Methodists. His reply astounded them.

"Twould be better to go to the Bryanites than go to hell!' He went on, more and more loudly, denouncing their behaviour and their blasphemy.

'Hold thy tongue, Billy, or go and roar somewhere else. We've had enough of 'ee for one night.'

Billy looked round, his face distorted with misery instead of lit by mischievous humour. 'You would roar out, too, if you felt my load. And roar I shall until I get it off!' This was Bunyan's Christian in *The Pilgrim's Progress* rather than his *Visions of Heaven and Hell*. He pushed the door open, and trudged out into the night, the mist which shrouded the scarred countryside lit here and there by fires at the pit-heads. But, though he laboured along the rough track as if he did indeed have Pilgrim's burden on his shoulders, he walked straight. Tonight there was no danger of his falling down an unfenced pit-shaft or crumpling into the ditch. He opened the door of his cottage and went in.

Joey looked up, astonished. 'You're home early, Billy ... early for a pay-night. Didn't you go to the kiddleywink?'

'Yes, I went. And come out as soon as I went in, almost.'

Incredulously she listened to his voice. 'You're not drunk. This is the first time you've come home sober on a pay-night all the years we've been married.'

'And for years before that,' added the little man. His flat voice took on an edge of determination as he went on. 'You will never see me drunk again, neether, by the help of the Lord.' He looked round the kitchen. There was no supper, for he never had need of anything to eat when he fell in through the door, dead drunk, on pay-nights. He did not, however, seem to notice, but went towards the stairs. Joey heard him go into the bedroom, and the door closed. When she went up he was kneeling by the bed.

On the Saturday he did not go to work. 'I'm going to wrestle till I find mercy,' he told Joey and, with the Bible and

Wesley's hymn-book, trudged up the stairs once more. She left him undisturbed, apart from calling him for dinner, but he was in no mood for food and she heard him moving about, thumping down onto his knees, 'roaring' in unaccustomed prayer, all this punctuated by the sound of his reading – the steady drone as he read the Bible alternating with the rhythmic cadences of the hymns he had heard as a boy. Now and again his voice rose as if in pain.

'What are you doing, Billy?' Joey shouted up the low flight of stairs.

'Crying for mercy!' he answered. For Billy the phrase was literally exact. 'Crying' meant both weeping and shouting, sometimes both together. But by the end of the day he showed only signs of emotional exhaustion instead of peace of mind.

'Go to bed, Billy,' his wife urged him.

'Yes, so I will.' He took off his top-clothes and dropped on the hard pallet. 'But I shall do as I said in the ale-house. Tomorrow I shall go and seek out the Methodists. They have a meeting in the morning.'

Sunday morning came with mist-filled skies and the driving rain that so often beats across west Cornwall in November. It did not deter Billy. In the same clothes he wore to the mine he set off for the little Bible Christian chapel and the Sunday morning class meeting, the fellowship group in which all Methodists, whatever branch of that church they belonged to, were expected to share their sins and triumphs. Here he would find those who would pray with him till he found peace.

An hour later, after tramping through the sludgy tracks for two miles, he was back again. 'Nobody came,' he muttered in angry frustration. 'Rain wouldn't keep *me* home if I had what they're supposed to have. I shall never join *there*!' He dropped his wet coat by the door and went back upstairs, where his Bible and hymn-book lay on the bed.

The rest of Sunday passed like the day before, and so did

Monday morning. In the afternoon he was due to work his 'core' at the mine and his fellow tinners looked at him askance. This was not the man they knew. No quips, no jokes, no gibes – only a lined and tired face, as if he had not slept through the whole weekend, and a constant rumble beneath his breath as he chipped away with his pick at the hard rock. Only one word was audible, and that came again and again.

'Mercy! . . . Mercy! . . . Mercy!'

There seemed no mercy, or at least only the hint and never the certainty of it. His journal records the same praying, reading, anguishing, through Monday and Tuesday, when he again worked his afternoon shift, and Wednesday morning until he went back below ground at two o'clock.

One fact horrified him as he looked back on those terrible days. Almost all the men in the Twelveheads district worked at the mine, either below or above ground. His own condition was soon known to everybody, and not only in the mine where he worked. But, as he records, not a single man amongst them spoke a word of hope or witness to him through those long days. Wesleyans and Bible Christians left him to find his way alone, or to fall by the wayside. Perhaps it was not surprising. He had mocked so many of them so often that they were hesitant to counsel him, much less offer to pray with him. He understood well enough why they kept away from him. But he never forgot. Such 'cowardice' would never characterise Billy himself. He would speak without hesitation even when he knew he would probably be rebuffed. 'Witness' was to be a reiterated theme in his preaching throughout his life.

Billy had not only a literal mind in his reading and interpretation of the Bible, but a very pictorial vision of what he read. The devil was as real to him as to Martin Luther, and he would easily have understood the old German reformer flinging his inkwell at Satan across the room. In his own way he did so in the mine-level that Wednesday afternoon.

41

'*You'll* never find mercy. You're too deep sunk in sin!' He seemed to hear the mocking words ring round the pit.

Billy crashed his pick against the granite wall. '*You're a liar, devil*!'

As he shouted, the words echoed along the level and he seemed to feel the burden lift from his shoulders. The struggle was over.

Back above ground as they climbed out of the narrow shaft he turned to his workmates. 'Sooner than go back to sin again, I would be put in that plat (open space) there and burned to death!' He began to shout with happiness as his fellows laughed, amused at this new turn in their excitable comrade's behaviour but uneasy and already awkward in his presence.

Long years afterwards Billy looked back on those hours following his deliverance. His vivid comment is both typical and memorable. 'They said I was a *mad*-man, but they meant I was a *glad*-man, and, glory be to God, I have been glad ever since!'

Climbing up from the mine, having thrust away the devil and his despairing temptations, Billy had a great sense of relief – but it was not yet the overwhelming joy that characterised the years that followed. That, however, was not far off. He reached home, as usual, about eleven o'clock and told Joey what had happened.

'You wouldn't eat supper all this week because you thought you were going to hell,' she said. 'Will you eat it now you're going to heaven?'

'No,' said Billy. 'I shall go and pray. I've found peace but I still want to find the joy of it.' He dropped his coat and went upstairs quietly – but not for long. His own account of what happened is simple and convincing.

'I said to the Lord, "Thou hast said, *They that ask shall receive, they that seek shall find, and to them that knock the door shall be opened* . . . and I have faith to believe it!" In an instant the Lord made me so happy that I cannot express

42

what I felt. I shouted for joy. I praised God with my whole heart for what he had done for a poor sinner like me, for I could say, The Lord hath pardoned all my sins.

'This was in November 1823, but what day of the month it was I do not know.

'But I remember *this*! Everything looked new to me, the people, the fields, the cattle, the trees. I was like a man in a new world.'

For Billy, this new awareness of God, this joy in the world – scarred as it was by mines, engine-houses, poverty and squalor – had one overwhelming result. He was the old, gay, witty, exuberant miner once again ... the man who could not keep quiet ... the man who would rather run than walk, dance than run, and sing than speak. But now his humour had a new roundness to it, his gaiety a new depth and his talk a new subject which he never forgot.

'I was a new man altogether. I told all I met what the Lord had done for my soul. I have heard some say that they have had hard work to get away from their companions, but I sought mine out – and had hard work to find them soon enough to tell them what the Lord had done for me. ... Some said they would have me back next pay-day. But, praise the Lord they have not got me yet.'

'I have been glad ever since.'

5

The New Man

A famous eighteenth-century wit, Sidney Smith, suggested that instead of 'bishops, priests and deacons', the traditional ministerial orders of the Church of England should be renamed 'Nimrods, ramrods and fishing-rods' because their consuming interests were hunting, shooting and fishing rather than the care of souls. There had been a considerable change by the end of the century – and the gibe was never entirely justified – but in too many parishes the Anglican clergy were casual if not lazy, and not a few were heavy drinkers if not dissolute. In Cornwall, particularly, despite the new turnpike roads and easier communication with the rest of England, change did not come rapidly. 'Methodism' had become the accepted 'Church' amongst the poor, and the miners, small holders and fishermen were to be found within it rather than in the Established Church.

But Methodism, after the turn of the century, had its own increasingly hardening establishment. There was a sharp division between ministers and laymen, who had little real power in their own Church. Discipline was more likely to be applied to those who challenged authority than to those who neglected the class-meeting or the Communion Service, which Wesley had regarded as central to the life of the Methodist 'societies'. With a large number of chapels under the care of each minister there was too little time for concentrated pastoral care and perhaps even less for aggressive evangelism. In the opinion of not a few younger men Wesley's Methodism had lost its sense of mission and had grown stale. One sign of this was that, despite its undoubted strength, there were many places – in Cornwall and Devon, for instances – where Methodist preaching had still never been heard.

In north Cornwall a boy named William O'Bryan was born in 1778 and John Wesley himself had once laid his hand on the boy's head and prayed: 'May he be a blessing to hundreds and to thousands!' O'Bryan was a gifted man – he spoke with power, and had considerable skill as an artist and engraver – but he was also a strong individualist, prepared to challenge authority if he thought he ought. One such challenge was that he began to preach, after his conversion – and preached wherever he thought right! For the most part his choice of place was where there had not been any other Methodist preaching, but this did not soften the cold anger of his superintendent minister. 'Mr O'Bryan will preach where *I* choose to plan him and nowhere else', was his attitude. Head-on clashes were inevitable.

As O'Bryan preached throughout north Cornwall and Devon, his following grew and so did his alienation from Wesleyan Methodism. He was expelled, received back and expelled again. In 1815, at Shebbear in Devon, 'The Bible Christians' came into existence, and became in effect, a separate Methodist denomination.

With surprising speed, partly because of their spiritual conviction, partly through their uninhibited expression of evangelical faith, and partly because they seemed to be recapturing what traditional Methodism had lost, they spread throughout the West Country, the South of England, the Isle of Wight and into London itself. Inevitably they were seen as competitors with the Wesleyan chapels, and not infrequently the building of 'Bryanite' chapels – despite their official title Cornwall preferred for a century or more to use

45

the old personalised name – meant they gained dissentients from the Wesleyan societies.

One of the earliest 'Bryanite' strongholds was in west Cornwall, where a man named Boyle had separated himself from the Wesleyans and gathered a following for a freer form of worship and evangelisation in a wide area round Truro and the western mining districts. Almost as soon as the Bible Christians became an acknowledged denomination Boyle and his followers joined them, thus gaining a new strength and coherence. They offered the very emphases which these dissatisfied Wesleyans were seeking. One of their strongest centres was the small mining village of Hicks Mill, on the edge of the United Mines near St Day, and only a mile or so from Billy Bray's home at Twelveheads.

The significance of this piece of Methodist history, unhappy though it was at the time, is that only in such a charismatic community as the Bible Christians could Billy Bray have fully expressed his own particular kind of experience or begun his own individual type of ministry. It seems safe to say that he would have been inhibited by the greater decorum of Wesleyan Methodism, probably disciplined by his ministers, and quite possibly expelled for his chapel-building activities. But, within the Bible Christian fold, he was at home and was immediately able to go out as a shepherd to seek the wanderers and the lost.

It is nevertheless greatly to the credit of Methodism in Cornwall that, even when another new Methodist denomination, the Primitive Methodists, established themselves in Cornwall, Methodism in all its branches was large-hearted enough to accept him and to tolerate, if it did not always officially welcome, his eccentricities and his exuberant spirit.

It was to Hicks Mill chapel that Billy went immediately after his conversion and, if there were any who suspected that his new experience might be short-lived (as in many cases, it frequently was), there was rejoicing over a notorious sinner reclaimed.

'Billy Bray is converted!'

The news spread throughout the whole district as quickly as water in a mine.

Nothing could have given him greater joy than the fact that his wife, Joey, went with him, perhaps awkwardly enough as one who had drifted away from her Christian profession, and at Hicks Mill, within a week of his own conversion, she had regained her own joyous experience. She was to remain his staunchest helper – and he must often have tried her patience – until her death.

Billy could not contain himself. He had to tell everybody he met about his experience and his principal area of witness was naturally the mine where he worked. There were plenty of men who were ready to laugh at him, as they had for so long laughed with him. There was contempt for his weakness in deserting his old, wild ways. There was certainly resentment that he, who had shared their drinking, their salacious story-telling and their jeers at religion, should now be preaching at them wherever he found them. But that was not the whole story.

'I had spent my time telling lies to make fun' of religious people and their ways 'but now I could tell them a new tale about heavenly truths, and what the Lord had done for me.'

Whatever had been done for him, he was a different man. So much was obvious. And 'it was not long before some of them were as mad as I was!'

Had he really given himself time to consider what he was doing it might have been more difficult. He was challenging the accepted code by which religious men got on with their work, went to chapel when they could, and did not interfere with the rights of others to say what they would and do what they wanted in return for a quiet life. Billy did not want a quiet life. 'There were men who were converted before I was but did not love the Lord enough to own him.' What was worse, in Billy's eyes, 'they did not love us enough to pray with us and tell us we were going to hell ... There was nobody who prayed in the mine where I worked.'

With Billy's radical change of heart and behaviour there came a change in the atmosphere. 'He gave me the power to pray with the men before we went to our different places of work.' While most of this took place with the men on his own 'core' who worked with him in the particular mine-level they had bid for, others certainly listened. The simplicity of his words and his strength of conviction were compelling. Mining was a dangerous occupation. A footslip on the ladder, a careless blow on the rock or not paying attention to the ominous sound of cracking in the low roof of the level where men worked almost doubled-up as they chipped at the granite face – any of these things could mean death. And death was not uncommon. Billy prayed for his companions. 'Lord if any of us must be killed today, let it be *me*. Let not one of these men die, for they are not happy. But I am, and if I die today I shall go to heaven.' He prayed on his knees, and when he rose from the red earth he would see tears in their eyes or running down their dark faces. 'Soon after,' he could record joyfully, 'some of them became praying men, too.'

His journal names some of these companions. There was old William, who would be moved to tears but soon afterwards would be swearing at his son as violently as ever. 'I was tempted not to pray with him again', says Billy, after constant failures to 'get him converted' but 'thank the Lord I did not yield to the temptation, and before the old man died he was made very happy in Jesus.'

There was Justin, who was with him in his unregenerate Devonshire days, shared his drunken frolics and now worked with him in the same 'core' in the Cornish mine. Billy's fellows made no secret of their contempt for his new life. 'You're a fool, Billy,' they would jeer. 'Just think what you're missing.' The sneering and the persecution went on constantly for if, here and there, a few took him seriously, the majority were angered and embarrassed by the intensity of his passion to change their lives. If he would not let them alone, they would certainly not leave him alone either. 'Leave that man alone!' shouted Justin. 'I knew him when he was a drunkard, and now he is a good man.' Then, more tenuously, 'I wish I was like him myself!'

Soon afterwards Billy buttonholed Justin as they went to work. 'I've got good news for you, Justin, my dear. I was down on my knees praying in the field where I was planting potatoes ... praying for *you*. And the Lord spoke to my mind. He said "I will save him soon." And so he will!'

It was not long before Justin came to the same experience. None too soon, Billy confides in his journal, for soon afterwards he fell fatally ill.

But, rich as he soon believed himself to be in spiritual things, he was poor enough in material ones. What he had earned had gone to the beer-shop in large measure and his wife had been fortunate if she found enough in his pocket, when he reeled home on pay-day, to pay for the few essentials on which they lived. The thin earth with its rocky outcrops and its poor soil grew little more than potatoes and meat was scarce even when there was money to buy it. In Cornwall, like Ireland, potatoes were the staple diet. He was never to know affluence throughout his life and even when he brought his wage home instead of spending it at the alehouse he was more apt to give part of it away to those more needy than himself than to bring it all to his wife. He had an assurance, typical of those who had a strong faith in God's personal interest, that 'the Lord would provide' – and, by his own account, this often happened as some of the stories will show. But, at this stage, immediately after his conversion his wife and family, like himself, had hardly anything in the larder, nothing in reserve and little more than the clothes they wore.

For Billy himself, 'clothes' meant, in addition to the clothes he wore down the mine, a well-worn pair of trousers and a fustian jacket – cotton cloth, dyed a drab colour which had faded with constant washing and showed the evidence of Joey's mending at the elbows. Billy was not worried about his jacket when he made his way to Hicks Mill chapel. The Lord looked on the heart and not on what a man was, or wore outside. There may well have been a few 'respectable' people in this Bible Christian stronghold but undoubtedly few of those who attended would have looked askance at Billy's jacket. They were mostly poor miners and farmworkers who shared his own difficulties in making ends meet.

Hicks Mill was his spiritual home from the beginning, and he could not help but be seen and heard. Before long, he would express himself with an exuberance of behaviour and a vividness of speech that his congregations would find unforgettable. But, in these months that followed his change of heart, the idiosyncrasies which were to become the basis of 'the Billy Bray legend' were still in the future. For the moment two matters filled his mind. The first was personal witness to the people he knew best, his fellow-miners and his immediate neighbours. The second was more inward – he knew he had an experience of God's overflowing love in Christ but he wanted much more. He believed that he was only on the fringe of the ocean, and any Cornishman knew very well that the shoals swam in deeper water than that. Even a 'farmer' whose only patch was the rocky ground in which he grew potatoes realised that shallow earth produced poor crops; good harvests came from good, deep soil. Billy was shrewd enough to know that natural laws also held in the spiritual world. To 'begin' was simple; it was the continuing that would determine whether he was truly 'saved'.

This, indeed, was Billy's criticism of many of the Methodists he knew. He was not so brash as to deny that they had a personal experience, but why did they not witness to him in his evil ways? Why had they not buttonholed him and tried to share what they had? It seemed as if they had been afraid to do so ... uncertain whether their experience was strong enough to stand up to his gibes and his salty, salacious wit. Already it was clear to Billy that a man should be able to 'speak to his experience', and that in a year's time he should have more to speak of than he had now. He must grow in grace.

Within a month or two of his conversion both these viewpoints came together in a single clarifying moment. Washed and tidy he made his way through the old mine-workings from Twelveheads to Hicks Mill. It was a Sunday morning and he was going to the class-meeting which met before worship. The Bible Christians had seen new reality breathed into this almost century-old Methodist institution. Gathered in the little chapel the members were expected to respond to the call of the class-leader and speak relevantly about their present experience in relation to their everyday life. In this case a stranger was leading the class.

The leader turned to one member. 'Can you truly say that Christ has cleansed you from all sin?'

The man remained silent.

'Not just from sin, but from *all* sin?' persisted the leader.

Billy was Methodist enough, right through his childhood, to know the terminology of Methodist belief. 'Redemption' and 'justification by faith' had been familiar phrases in his grandfather's home. But this was something more. The word rolled through his mind, blotting out the leader's conversation.

'This is *sanctification*,' he said to himself. 'Not just to be cleansed from the guilt of what I've done all through those years here and in Devon ... but to be held against the *power* of sin.' He was in a world of his own, and the chapel benches and the men on each side were forgotten. He swung round off the bench and thumped down on his knees as if he were at home.

'Lord,' he muttered, and to him it seemed as if he were shouting aloud, 'I want this blessing. I want it here and now.'

A moment or two later he was back in his place and the

51

leader, going along the row, pointed his finger at Billy. 'What have you to say, Mr Bray?'

Billy described what had happened. 'And the Lord said to me, "Billy, thou art clean through the word I have spoken unto thee." And I said to him, "Lord, I believe it." Four months ago I was a great sinner against God. Since that time I have been justified by his grace. *And while I have been here this morning the Lord has sanctified me wholly!*'

The leader looked at him, almost through him.

'If you can believe it, it is so.'

'I *can* believe it,' answered Billy.

The meeting over he set off for home, crossing the narrow-gauge rails which took the trucks of ore away from the mines. At home he told Joey what had happened. 'And over the railroad, and all the way home, all around me seemed so full of glory that it dazzled my sight. I had a joy unspeakable, and full of glory!'

It was a sign that this little miner's Christian experience had not stopped where it began, with his conversion, but was to go on growing deeper as the years passed.

'Glory' was to become one of his most typical and reiterated expressions.

But there were to be tensions and difficulties, too. He was to be faced with a dilemma about Sunday-observance which would test his experience and his integrity very quickly.

Sunday, in most cases, was a 'free' day. The mines were not working. The religious part of the population went to class-meeting and worship, the rest lounged about and talked, slept off Saturday night's carousal or went to the beer-shops. There was little else to do in an area entirely without other attractions. But many of these west Cornwall mines, especially in the lower levels, suffered from water seepage. If the water was not pumped off on Sunday it would be impossible to work on Monday and, in the mine where Billy worked, the levels filled with water every twelve hours if they were not pumped free. Every Sunday, therefore, someone had to spend part of the day drawing the water to the surface.

On the Sunday when Billy's turn came round he was at Hicks Mill chapel. Whether he had forgotten about his duty, which seems unlikely, or whether he intended to spend a while at the chapel and then get back to it, he had a tug-of-war going on within himself. As always he could put it into words afterwards.

'I said, "What shall I do, Lord?"'

'And the Lord said, "Stay here and worship me!"'

'So I said, "I will, Lord . . . and the water can find its own way out!"'

But there were no miracles that day, as Billy found when he reached the mine at six o'clock on Monday morning. The mine captain was in a furious temper.

'Why weren't you here yesterday? Gone back to drinking, have you?'

'No.' Billy looked up at him with an untroubled face. 'It is the Lord's will that I should not work on Sundays!'

The captain exploded, his face getting redder as he went on. 'I'll give you "the Lord's will", Bray! You're finished here, from this moment!'

Billy turned away to go home, surprisingly at peace in his mind. He 'had the Lord of the rocks and hills for his friend, and did not care who was against him'. But his peace was broken when one of his friends on the same 'core' told him that he, too, had been sacked, presumably because they were both supposed to be on duty and the other man could not do the work by himself.

'That's all wrong,' said Billy. 'You shouldn't be turned away on my account. It was my fault and I'll go to the captain and tell him so.'

The manager was in a quieter mood when Billy went back. 'But you must give up this notion about not working on Sundays. Men *have* to work if the mine is to be kept in working order. The water's got to be got away!'

The little miner was as stubborn as ever. 'I know you're the master here, but I've got a new Master now. He tells me I must not work on the Sabbath-day but keep it holy. And I shall do as he tells me!' He was not surprised when the mine-manager waved him away and went across to talk to his accounts-clerk. Billy waited while they talked, but caught one comment from the clerk.

'If I had the same experience as Bray I wouldn't work on Sunday, either!'

His workmates were astounded, though on reflection Billy was not – for was not the Lord of the rocks and hills his friend? – when the captain told him he would make sure that he need not work on Sundays in that mine again. More, he had been enquiring about this change of heart and the way he did his work during the week. Not only need he not work on Sundays. 'I'll have a look at the work-sheets and arrange for you to be free to go to your chapel at Hicks Mill, or wherever you go, in the evening during the week as well!'

That day, not only the mine-pitted landscape but the very levels of the mine where he was at work were 'full of glory unspeakable'.

6

On the Plan

It was as well for Billy's peace of mind that Captain Hosken had had that sudden change of heart, making him free of work in the evenings as well as on Sundays. The actual chore he had been given instead was not, in itself, very exciting. He was put to work on the surface instead of below ground, humping a heavy barrow to move ash and that paid a good deal less money than he would have earned with his pick in the deep levels of the mine. Its compensation, however, was that he could go when he wished to his beloved Hicks Mill chapel. And, just at this moment, there was good reason for his presence in chapel, though not at Hicks Mill.

Soon after his own conversion, and perhaps not unconnected with it, a 'revival' had broken out in Twelveheads, based on the Wesleyan chapel there not far from his own home – presumably the building which had succeeded the small chapel his grandfather had built. If it had been a choice between the Lord's work and the mine captain's work there is no doubt which it would have been. Now he was uninhibited in his decision to give all the time he could to praying, speaking, pleading with those who came.

For the Twelveheads Methodists it was an uneasy period. Their Wesleyan staidness was more than a little disturbed by the cries of sinners under conviction and their even louder shouts of praise as they found an assurance of forgiveness.

Billy shouted in triumph with the loudest of them. It seemed to him that he was 'much wanted'. Those who worshipped there regularly included some of the very men who had made no kind of witness in the mine when he most needed it. Their own profession of faith was, however, not merely silent. 'The old professors were very dead at that time, and would come into the chapel with their hats under their arm, and look very black at us.' Billy's word 'us' must have included a number of those whose conversion had been stimulated by his own tumultuous experience and his uninhibited witness at the mine. They were not to be put off by criticism of their rumbustious evangelism. The revival meetings went on long into the night, and night after night.

'The Lord was with us, and soon tore a hole in Satan's kingdom. We had, I think, nearly a hundred converted in that one week, the first week I ever worked all the time for the Lord in his house.'

Friday was 'taking-on' day at the mine, and if he were to work, and earn any money, he must go and join the queue of men to whom the mine captain apportioned their tasks for the coming month. 'Earthly gold' had become of small value compared with 'heavenly treasure', and he decided to let 'taking-on' day go by. He would stay where he was and 'work for the Lord'. How Joey would make ends meet he did not even consider.

It was in the evening that two men walked up to the chapel and stood outside. They were not candidates for conversion, but messengers from the mine.

'Tell Billy Bray we do want to see him.'

Billy got up from his knees and went outside.

'Captain Hosken have sent us to say that he have appointed you to work in 'chapel shaft', Billy. A good place it is, too. Better than you do deserve!'

Billy went back inside. This was the Lord's doing, he concluded. On the Monday morning, after a strenuous weekend of evangelism, he went 'to see the place the Lord had provided'. It was, in truth, better than he had had before. In the level where he had been working when he had chosen to stay at chapel on Sunday rather than go and empty the mine-water he had been earning two pounds a month. In this new shaft he would be earning five pounds instead.

'Praise the Lord!' shouted Billy as he climbed down the shaft. He shouted it again as he climbed to the surface when his shift was over. And at home, to Joey, he said 'I didn't have to work near so hard as I did in the other shaft ... I got three pounds a month more ... I can do the Lord's work all day on Sunday ... and I can do the Lord's will which is better than all the money in the world!'

It was not to be the last time that Joey wished the Lord had given her husband a measure of common sense as well as a burning heart. Money, or the lack of it, would often be almost as much of a problem as it was when he spent it in the beerhouse on his way home from work. Yet nothing could dissuade this large-hearted little man from his assurance that even if he gave it all away the Lord would still ensure that Joey and the children never went short.

Experience, Joey had to admit, often proved him right.

It was about a year after his conversion that he felt impelled to go beyond the ordinary limits of an ardent church-member. Witnessing in the mine and helping in a revival was not enough. The Lord seemed to be calling him to a larger ministry. He joined the little band of 'exhorters' – men, and in some cases women, who were permitted to 'exhort their hearers to repent and turn to God'. It was a limited but recognised function which served two purposes. It allowed those who did not have all the qualities for preaching and the conduct of worship to exercise a real ministry of the sort prized by the Bible Christian Church. but it also served as a training-ground for those who would eventually take their place 'on the plan'.

All Methodist chapels were grouped into 'circuits' consisting of a large number of 'societies', the Methodist term for the membership of a local chapel. Ministers were appointed to have charge of a circuit, with pastoral charge either of the whole circuit or, if there were more than one minister, of a number of chapels. But because, while a minister could exercise pastoral care of a number of chapels and conduct their business meetings, he could obviously not preach in more than two or three on the same Sunday, Methodism in all its branches, made full use of lay-preachers. The 'circuit plan' listed the ministers and lay-preachers and, setting out all the chapels in the circuit, noted the preachers appointed to them by the superintendent minister for the forthcoming quarter. A lay-preacher did not, at that period, have to undertake any training or to pass examinations, but did have to convince the ministers and the other preachers of his 'call to preach'. He must have the 'gifts and graces', as the Methodist phrase went, which would make him an acceptable preacher of the gospel.

Billy Bray's graces were not of any aristocratic kind, though he often referred to himself as 'the King's son'. Grace, for him, was from above. But of his gifts there was already no doubt whatever.

His name was 'put on the plan' as a preacher in 1824, about a year after his conversion.

He was not a wide reader, despite the effect of Bunyan's *Visions* in the last stage of his unregenerate days. The two books he did read, constantly and fully, were the Bible and the Methodist hymn-book. How was he to set about 'making a sermon'? Not by sitting down and making lengthy notes – that was evident to all who heard him – but by meditating on the word of God, on his own experiences and on other people's, and by a quick-witted assessment of the world as he saw it.

The fustian jacket was no proper dress for a preacher, and he came to adopt the tidy black suiting, with a white tie, which marked him as a serious and sober man committed to leading worship. Nothing could have been less indicative of what the congregation might expect! True, in his eyes, most things were either black or white and he had no patience with compromise. But, for the rest, he was the most highly-coloured personality in the Cornish pulpits for the thirty years after he was put 'on the plan'.

A famous preacher of the last century, the Rev Mark Guy Pearse, himself a Cornishman, has left a fine description of him in his prime.

'If you had overtaken Billy on the way you could not have long been in doubt as to who he was. A little, spare, wiry man ... the sharp, quick, discerning eye that looked out from under the brows, the mouth almost hard in its decision, all the face softened by the light that played constantly upon it, and by the happy wrinkles round the eyes, and the smile that had perpetuated itself – these belonged to no ordinary man. And with the first suspicion that that was Billy Bray there would quickly come enough to confirm it. If you gave him half a chance there would certainly be a straight-forward question about your soul, in wise, pithy words. And if the answer was what it should be, the lanes would ring with his happy thanksgiving.'

Dr Pearse's comments about happy wrinkles and a smile, about pithy words and the lanes ringing with his rejoicing give essential clues to the power that this man had, almost from the very beginning, over his hearers.

He seldom began with a text, though he would range through the whole Bible in his exposition. Instead, he would probably start the sermon with the verse of a hymn. Or he might plunge straight into some recent experience of his own. From then on he was not confined by the first, second and third points of conventional preachers. He spoke 'as the Lord gave him'. The chapel could rock with laughter at one moment, only to find their amusement turned on themselves as he pointed a moral that stabbed their consciences. His illustrations were homely, right out of the everyday experience of the people in front of him.

With a diet of bread and potatoes, for the most part, and little enough meat, these people could at any rate tell good bread from bad. To Billy 'the Bread of Life' was real bread. 'Precious loaf this is!' he cooed as he spoke about Jesus as the bread of life. 'The patriarchs and prophets ate of this loaf and never found a hard bit of crust about it! The apostles and martyrs ate of this bread, too, for many years and never found a bit of husk in it! And, bless the Lord, poor old Billy Bray can eat it and when he gets to be an old man without teeth he will get fat on it!'

At the time of a parliamentary election he preached on the subject of Christ's entry into Jerusalem and, in vivid phrases, pictured the crowds shouting 'Hosanna to the Son of David' as they danced and flung the palm branches in front of the donkey. He went on to describe the enthusiasm of local men, half-drunk on money provided by the parliamentary candidate's agents, shouting 'John Smith for ever!'

'Who is to say to Billy Bray, then,' he asked, 'that he shall not shout "Jesus for ever!" without anyone finding fault with him?'

He could not understand those who decried his exuberance as though shouting and dancing and excitement had no place in proclaiming the good news. In our own time the break-out from conventional, contained church worship which has brought a note of immediacy and an element of freedom into congregational worship and group-sharing is sometimes criticised as emotional, a new but transient phase. On the other hand it has been defended as a recovery of past freedom, a necessary expression of deeply-felt emotions. Billy Bray faced the same criticisms but found them narrow and groundless. If he wanted to shout 'Long live Jesus' he saw no reason why he should refrain from doing so.

But, alongside the uninhibited outbursts which he could not keep out of his sermons his words were often very sharply pointed and, because he spoke out of a life shared with his hearers, the thrusts went home. As they did, for instance, in his illustration about the 'two mines'.

His congregation was made up of tin-miners, for the most part, who knew the two mines very well. They worked in one or other of them. The more fortunate were in a good mine with plenty of tin and copper ore which was coming out easily. This meant that, in their case, wages were good and seemed likely to remain so. The other was, like many of the Cornish mines, a hard and unprofitable place. Ore-yields were low, working conditions were more cramped than usual and, because the 'adventurers' who had put their money into sinking the shaft were getting little return for their investment, the miners' wages were low too.

'Let's say I work in Wheal Misery,' says Billy (it is impossible to reproduce the dialect and vocabulary he used, though Cornishmen can easily reconstruct it!), 'and I have to nearly break my back to get any tin at all down there. Even when I've got it it isn't worth heaving to the surface. But that don't matter to me, for on pay-day I do go over to Wheal Profit and stand in with the men who work there to get my wages. When 'tis my turn to hold my hand for my money before the manager what do 'ee think he'll say to me?'

There is a roar of laughter. They know the manager – and know what sort of language he would use.

'Don't you work over to Wheal Misery, then?'

The miner shuffles unhappily. 'Yes,' he admits.

'Then go over there for your wages and don't think you can cheat me by coming over here for better money.'

'As I slink away with my tail between my legs,' says Billy, 'I hear what he says. "If you do want Wheal Profit wages you must come and work in Wheal Profit mine!"'

'And so it is in heavenly things,' he goes on. 'If you want Christ's wages when the heavenly pay-day comes you have to serve Christ now. But if you persist in serving the Devil now, 'tis the Old Devil who will pay you your wages when the settling-day comes around.'

The point was made and the laughter banished. Solemnity reigned in the hushed chapel.

But it would not be long before some quip came again and the laughter-lines round his dark eyes crinkled as he rattled on to make another telling point.

Apart from his inability to remain serious for long while he preached, or at any rate to maintain an equable decorum, the services he took seem to have been reasonably unexcited. But it was very different afterwards. The actual service of worship ended with an invitation to stay for the 'after-meeting'. In particular those who had been moved to change their ways and seek forgiveness and salvation were urged to remain. Now came a much more uninhibited and unrestrained atmosphere. Free prayer came from the congregation, sometimes from more than one at once. Ejaculations rose from everywhere. 'Glory', Hallelujah' and 'Praise the Lord' were the commonest of them – though this sort of response was common in worship, too, and prayers and sermons were punctuated by shouts of praise and agreement through the whole congregation. Prayer for sinners who showed signs of wanting to change their ways were intimate and personalised.

As time passed men and women who were under conviction groaned aloud and those who prayed for and with them raised their voices to be heard, for this was no carefully ordered gathering in which only one could pray at a time. All over the chapel there were men and women praying, louder and louder, in their rhythmic Cornish phraseology, unintelligible to any outsider. Here and there the groans and agony of struggle changed to shouts of triumph as peace and release came to a burdened man. And with the shouts of the forgiven sinner came the accompanying song and shout of triumph from those who had been praying with him. As emotion rose higher and the one sinner reclaimed became two or three or a dozen, so the restraints were progressively discarded. To a stranger, and especially a critical visitor, the whole scene would have seemed devoid of decency, decorum and order, and the atmosphere to be one of orgiastic frenzy. There were plenty of people who condemned it as such.

Criticism was directed most of all at Billy himself, because in the midst of all the singing, praying and shouting he was the most conspicuous figure. He prayed louder than any, shouted and sang at the top of his not inconsiderable voice. But he did more than this – he danced instead of walking. Jigging, leaping and prancing he dominated the whole after-meeting. And far from walking home exhausted, he seemed to dance out of the chapel as the last candles were blown out and those who were now quiet enough to hear the sounds of the night could hear his voice and his feet as he 'danced his way home', too exhilarated to keep his feet on the ground, his head out of the heavenly clouds or the shouts of praise from his lips.

To Billy, rejoicing in the 'victories' he had witnessed and shared in, joy was the supreme quality of religious experience.

And what could anyone do, when God was so good and his mercy so unconfined, but 'dance for joy'?

7

Dance for Joy

'For gracious sake, Billy, do 'ee stop capering about so!'

The little miner, small, spry, still with plenty of energy in his early thirties, seemed unable to keep still. In his unregenerate days – and they were not so long ago, as his workmates remembered very vividly – he could not stop talking. Even when he was hammering away at a crevice to push in an explosive that would blast the rock ahead of them he would be chattering over his shoulder. While they sat to eat their 'crowst', the Cornish word for a packed lunch which would almost certainly be a potato pasty, he would keep them laughing, sometimes even choking with laughter, with a wit that was irrepressible. His face, dull in repose, was seldom immobile. Usually, his grimaces and his gestures were as telling as his words.

Far from all being in the past, these idiosyncrasies were part of his continuing way of expressing himself. His stories were no longer salty and salacious, they had what he would have called 'a heavenly meaning'. He still talked as much as ever, but if he could not avoid the witticisms they were at the expense of evil, evil-doers and the devil himself. To his repertoire of extrovert behaviour there had been added song and prayer. But something else had been added too.

Billy, who could never keep silent, found that he also could not keep still!

'Capering about,' as they called it, was simply one more way, added to singing and shouting and praying, in which he could express his ecstatic sense of joy.

It was something that 'came upon him' very soon after his conversion. His feet would not keep to their old trudging tread on the way from his home to the mine. Because the terrible scenery – to other people a ghastly panorama of smoking chimneys, vapoury holes and open pitheads with clanking engines – was to him full of the glory of God he had to respond to this transformed landscape by leaping and jumping, instead of merely walking. And every time he leapt he shouted 'Glory!' or 'Hallelujah!' or 'Praise the Lord!'

At least it would surely have been different below ground? But it was not different at all. The tunnels were narrow and the rocky roof low and jagged with its outcropping granite, against which the miner's hat was some sort of slight protection. The hard ground was sludgy with dirty water which grew warmer, filthier and deeper the further a miner climbed down the shaft. But, to this sturdy, lithe little man, lack of breadth and height were no limitation. The love of God knew neither height, nor length, nor breadth nor depth – and he had to express it in all its unrestricted wonder.

'I could leap and dance for joy just as well underground as on the surface,' he commented later.

'My companions used to tell me that was no kind of religion – dancing, and singing and making so much to-do. But I was born in the fire and I couldn't live in the smoke!' Complaints were no use, even when the levels reverberated with his raised voice and leaping towards the low roof was a danger in itself. 'They said there was no need to leap and dance and make so much noise, for the Lord wasn't deaf, and he knows our hearts. Do you know what I said to these dull professors who were ashamed to speak about their faith?

'I said, "You know the devil isn't deaf, either, but that

don't stop his followers making a great noise. I've got more to shout about than they! The devil would rather see us doubting than shouting!"'

He grinned happily. 'I could feel the joy of the Lord two hundred and fifty fathoms below ground ... and that's getting on a long way down towards hell!'

About his experience and his expression of it there was something infectious. One of his close friends, with whom he had shared the danger of the Devon mines and the sins of the Devon ale-houses, was converted about the same time as himself, no doubt with some advocacy from Billy himself. John, however, went to the Wesleyan chapel while Billy was becoming a staunch Bible Christian. They 'came on the plan' together and John would sometimes come to hear Billy preach. But that was enough. The sermon over, John would leave. His Wesleyan austerity was affronted by the after-meeting.

'I can't stand all this praying and shouting and dancing, with everybody going on together. How do you think the Lord can understand what everybody is saying, all at once. 'Tis as noisy as an ale-house on pay-night!'

But John's staid view of religion was not proof against Billy's enthusiasm.

'The Lord spoke to him a dream,' said Billy. 'One Saturday night he had a dream that showed him he was foolish to speak against shouting when the Lord made his people happy. The next night, and ever afterwards, he stayed to the end, leaping with as much joy as I ever did myself.

'He was done with the doubters and was got up with the shouters.

'Praise the Lord!'

It was to be expected that Billy's sense of joy in religion characterised his preaching just as much as it did every other part of his life.

He knew his Bible quickly enough, and well enough, to find the passages that suited him.

'Listen to what it do say in the Psalms. "Thou has turned for me my mourning into dancing. Thou hast put off my sackcloth and girded me with gladness ... O Lord my God I will give thanks unto thee for ever."'

This would be followed by a string of similar quotations.

'Listen to what Jeremiah says – and he should know what he was talking about, for he had more than enough to put up with. "Then shall the virgin rejoice in the dance, both young man and old together, for I will turn their mourning into joy ..."'

His critics – and there were plenty of them, especially in the early days before he had become both a popular preacher and something of a Cornish Methodist folk-hero – would shake their heads. 'You got it all wrong, Billy, my son. It don't mean what it says. It don't really mean you got to dance ... not like people dance nowadays ... not capering about like you do!'

Billy would look dumbfounded. 'Don't the Bible mean what's written there, then? I don't know what it do say in *your* Bible, but I can tell 'ee what it says in *mine*. "David danced before the Lord *with all his might*!" And not only David the king, neither. "All the house of Israel brought up the ark of the Lord with shouting, and with the sound of a trumpet." What have 'ee got to say to that, then?' He would look round in mock astonishment, his bushy dark eyebrows raised in quirky interrogation.

'Are 'ee going to stand alongside Saul's daughter, Michal, who looked on David dancing before the Lord and despised him in her heart? If David had something to dance about and leap about because he was bringing back the ark of the Lord to where it did belong ... don't *we* have much more to dance and shout about than *he* did? Why, we've got the Lord himself!

'And do you know what we sing ... what Wesley wrote with his own hand?

67

> "True pleasures abound
> In the rapturous sound
> And my heart it doth dance at the sound of his name."

'If David could dance, and John Wesley could dance, why can't poor Billy Bray dance and shout?'

The critics were not always silenced. Like Billy's friend John, before his crossing from the 'doubters' camp' to the 'shouters' camp', they objected vehemently to the 'after-meetings' which followed the normal act of worship, and to the transition from order to confusion as Billy followed up his 'appeal' for conversion.

''Tis all so much uproar. Even if it says in the Scripture that David shouted that isn't no ground for everybody shouting all at once!'

Billy would cock his head on one side, looking as though he were taken aback by the criticism – as though it were the first time, not the hundredth, that he had heard it. His answers were not original, either, though he made them sound as though they were. 'Let me see, then ... Don't it say somewhere ... would it be in the Book of Ezra? ... would it be at the foundation of the Temple? I remember it now. "All the people shouted with a great shout, and the people could not discern the voice of the shout of joy from the noise of the weeping of the people, for the people shouted with a loud shout, *and the noise was heard afar off.*"

'If they could shout in the Lord's temple, should *we* not shout when our Lord gains the victory over the Old Devil? Don't you think *he* shouts when he loses one of those he thought was his own? And surely we should shout louder than *he*?'

Billy could always score off his critics, for he was less inhibited than they, and he could match their solemn antagonism with a sharp wit and a ready knowledge of the words of the Bible. He had no awareness that the context from which he drew his quotations might not be apposite to his purpose.

68

He must often have been less than fair to them, for the enthusiast, and not least the new convert, not infrequently fails to give due respect to an expression of faith that seems to him pedestrian or lacking in conviction. If something of the earlier vigour had gone out of Wesleyan Methodism, not least by comparison with the driving and youthful enthusiasm of the Bible Christians, it was still true that quieter ways of worship and a less ecstatic form of expression were often real, vital and meaningful. Nor were all the Bible Christians in favour of this apparently untrammelled excitement. They had great and powerful preachers, both ministers and lay people, men and women, who looked askance at what seemed unbridled behaviour which might well bring the gospel into disrepute.

In fact, had such methods been allowed to go without comment or constraint, and had they been widespread, they might easily have led to shallow if noisy displays of feeling without being indicative of any genuine depth of experience. There was, however, very little danger of this happening.

Billy was not the founder of a movement, though others shared or copied what he did. He was an individualist – more, he was a 'natural' in the sense that though others might share the powerful experience that was his, only he himself would be likely to express it genuinely in this way. He had, in short, his own 'charisma' – gifts that seemed, in his time, uniquely to belong to himself, that marked him out from other men and, before long, made him a household name throughout the whole of Cornwall.

It must be added that, because there was nothing false about him, his private face was the same as his public one. It was not only where others watched him, in the mine or the chapel, for instance, that he 'danced'. His wife knew it well enough, for she warned him to take care where he put his feet when 'joy' took hold of him when he rose from his prayers in the bedroom.

'If you leap about like that, Billy, you'll make a hole in

the floor and put your feet through the planchen' (the Cornish word for the planking covering the ceiling of the living-room, often wearing thin with the years).

It was some time later that Billy was talking to a friend. 'There are times when I get very happy. My soul gets full of glory and then what can I do but dance? I was home in my chamber (bedroom) the other day and one of those times came on me. The glory came streaming down on my soul. And do you know what happened?

'I danced so lustily that my heels went down through the planchen!'

There was no division between 'chapel behaviour' and 'home behaviour' to Billy. When his wife Joey regained her old experience at Hicks Mill chapel, a week after his own conversion, he must have danced all the way home. Certainly it is easy to see him, so full of happiness when he reached home, that he hugged her and then, bending down, put his arms round her and carried her round and round the little living-room. If you expressed your delight in that way at home, why not in chapel?

And Billy did. Alongside the singing and praying and dancing and shouting in the after-meeting went the 'carrying'. Short though he was, he had a tin-miner's muscles in his arms, and it was the most natural thing in the world for him to rush on a man who announced that he had 'found salvation,' bend down, heave him from his knees and carry him round the chapel in triumph.

But, to the more conventional onlookers – and most people were much more self-possessed than Billy – it must have come as a shock!

And, with uneasy noddings of the head, more than one must have said to another – 'I hope he don't never do that to *me*!'

Emphatically, Billy was no exhibitionist. He was a simple, good, lively man who could not contain the joy that flooded his soul, and never ceased to flood it as long as he lived.

'Simplicity' is the key-word to his character and achievements.

If he was uncomplicated in his behaviour and his reactions he was equally so in his faith, his generosity and his attitude to the Bible. Heaven was a reality, and so was hell. He was a man of his time in basing his vision of both on the picture-language of the scriptures. He believed in God and, in Bunyanesque imagery, in the devil, and he knew that by a miracle of grace he had been plucked from the devil's kingdom and brought into the Kingdom of God's Son. His belief in prayer was not only in a direct communication, verbal and immediate, between God and himself but also as an awareness of God, while he worked and walked, in the world about him. In the same way he accepted that if he did what God wanted, God would look after him – though he never interpreted this as meaning that he would be freed from sorrow, stress or even poverty. Because of the intensity of this faith he had no fear of death, which he saw as the entrance-gate of heaven, or of over-spending himself in generosity to people more needy than himself or in the service of his Master.

It must not be forgotten that he was, for the most part, preaching and speaking to people as uncomplicated as himself. In the growing towns there was a measure of wealth and, with that, went education (fairly limited even to the tradesmen in the 1820s and 1830s) and a measure of countrified sophistication. Cornwall, however, was still one of the remote parts of the country. Its gentry shared the social habits and activities of their class anywhere in Britain and travelled to London in their coaches for the seasonal joustings of the wealthy and their hangers-on, but that was a world that never spilled over in the life of the peasantry, the fishing villages or the mining communities. It is not possible for most of us to imagine the limitations within which Billy Bray and tens of thousands of his kind lived. The restrictions were physical – few, apart from soldiers, or miners going over the county border in Devon, would travel far from the place where they were born. The limitations were material, and even those who did not spend their meagre wages on ale had little spare money for extra possessions or 'fripperies'. They were mental – not many people today can realise how difficult it was to think widely or deeply where most of the population was illiterate, too poor to buy the occasional newspaper even if they could read it, and so unversed in affairs beyond their own county, or even their own neighbourhood, that 'local gossip' was, for them, the equivalent of 'knowledge of the world'.

Yet 'the world beyond the world' broke in. Billy could appeal to 'scripture' in his sermons because its images and phraseology were part of the Cornish inheritance over almost a century, since Wesleyan revivals and chapels, and not least Charles Wesley's familiar hymns, had turned them into common currency. Even the turns and usages of Cornish speech echoed Biblical language. This nearness of 'the world beyond' was reinforced by two matters, amongst others. One was the frequency of death, in the mines and amongst small children in particular. The other was Cornish superstition. Any visitor to west Cornwall today should easily understand how fully the strange-shaped boulders, the hut circles and cairns, the desolate moorland, would seem to be populated by 'spirits' to an unlettered people.

This was, in part, the context of Billy's ministry. His hearers were mostly people like himself, and he had only been lifted out of it when he was transferred to the ampler spiritual world in which God was his Father and heaven an ever-present experience.

His congregations, for intance, had no doubt that he believed in the reality of the devil for he had a place in so many of his sermons. Yet he never gave him much deference. He was the villain, but to those who held the sword of righteousness he was already a defeated villain.

'Why, he couldn't even get the better of poor old Billy!

He thought he'd got him in his grasp for ever and then, just as he was heating up the fire, Billy slipped right through his fingers! Some disgusted with hisself he was!'

Billy had a strange habit of talking about himself in the third person, creating a much more memorable visual image than by saying 'I'.

He knew the value of ridicule as a weapon in the struggle for men's souls. Though he had the language to paint the horrors of hell he was much more likely to turn sinners from their ways by urging the folly of serving so foolish a master. He trimmed the devil's claws and blunted his horns by mockery. He talked of 'the old devil' with patronising scorn. He was 'old smutty-face' and Billy laughed at him as the children laughed at the blacksmith smudged with the ash from his anvil fire. He was a loser in the end, however hard he tried. Had he not been turned out of heaven for presumption?

'The devil,' he said in one of his sermons, 'the devil said to me, "Billy, thou art a fool to go on preaching." Do you know how I got rid of him? I said, "Fool ... me? Not such a fool as thee! For thee was in a good situation and didn't know how to keep it!" *That* sent him running!'

For those who had 'situations' in some of the bigger houses it was an apt phrase.

Not that he underestimated the devil's persistence, his ultimate ploy against those who put off the day of decision. 'It is dangerous to put off our soul's salvation till we are in our death-beds, for where there is one who gets the prize there are ten that lose it ... and the same old devil that got in at them downstairs will get at them when they are in their beds.'

'The devil knows where I live' was a reiterated phrase in his sermons. 'He do try and get at me when I'm not looking. He's so cunning you got to be on the watch all the time.'

' "I'll have thee down to hell after all, Billy," the devil said to me,' so he reported in one sermon. 'Aw, will 'ee now?

Hast thee got a little lew (sheltered) place in hell where I could sing thee a song? I'll sing thee a song about Jesus Christ, and shout, and praise the Lord. And that's a sound thee hasn't heard in hell for fourteen years! How would 'ee like that, devil?'

It was not always as easy as it sounded to repulse temptation. Though he must have had few inclinations to go back to his old life he certainly suffered the ebb and flow of Christian experience and, like all those who 'dwell in the heights' there were moments when he plunged near to the depths. One such occasion brought him to an altercation as fierce as Bunyan's Christian had had with Apollyon.

Billy was coming home from the mine one night, the darkness lit only by the flares of the mines, the glow from the embers at the pit-heads and the dim light of the moon. It was night-time that always gave substance to the superstititions of west Cornwall. Along this track were shafts where there had recently been a number of accidents, either from carelessness or from men falling down unused shafts on their way from the ale-house. He passed the first one, though he felt himself almost irresistibly drawn towards it.

'The devil would have had me throw myself down it if he could.'

Near the second shaft he became convinced that the two men who had recently been killed in it would suddenly rise from it and confront him. It took all his courage to walk past it and not to break into a run.

Beyond the shaft was a narrow bridge over a stream of water running from the mines. On this bridge he would meet the devil himself. He knew it. In the dimness he could vaguely see the form of his waiting adversary. He shook all over. He could best the devil in verbal struggle but could he beat him in physical combat? The devil was strong enough to fling him off the bridge or hurl him down the shaft he had just passed with such fear.

Then the mists in his mind cleared, though the night stayed

dim as ever. 'The devil?' he muttered. 'Who is the devil, then? What can *he* do? He's a fallen angel, held in chains! And *I* am Billy Bray! God is my Father! Why should *I* fear the devil?'

He rushed the last few feet towards the bridge. 'Come on then, thou devil!' he yelled aloud. 'Come on, Lucifer and all the demons, I fear thee not!' His voice grew louder with his confidence. He stood in the middle of the narrow planks over the red stream. 'Come on, old ones and young ones, black ones and blue ones, fiery and red-hot ones! Come on, devil and all thy ugly hosts!'

There was silence except for the rattling of the waters over the stones below, and it was suddenly filled with the sound of Billy's voice, singing as he stood on the bridge.

'Jesus, the name high over all
In hell, or earth, or sky;
Angels and men before it fall,
And devils fear and fly!'

Strident voices came nearer, catching up with him as men ran past the deadly shafts. 'What's the matter with 'ee, Billy? Seen a ghost, have 'ee?'

'No,' answered Billy, 'but I nearly seen the devil.'

He stood on the bridge and told them what had happened.

8

'Bethel' and 'Three-eyes'

Billy's own three chapels were, for a century, amongst the best-known landmarks of west Cornwall's Bible Christians. They were landmarks, too, in his own spiritual growth and pilgrimage. Nothing in his story better illustrates his faith, his perseverance, his growing fame and, for that matter, his natural wit. At the same time they show that he was regarded both with respect on the one hand and with considerable scorn and hostility on the other.

The stories are told, at considerable length, in his own journal and quoted with great faithfulness by his first biographer, F. W. Bourne.

Prayer is the thread that links them all together.

Twelveheads itself had a small Wesleyan chapel. But the Bible Christians had only 'a little old house to preach in, which would hold twenty or thirty persons'. It served also as a Sunday-school and was used for the class-meetings. 'In the neighbourhood there were a great many dark-minded wicked people and the Lord put it into my mind to build a chapel.' Chapel building ran in the family, he remembered. His mother had a cottage and small-holding at Cross Lanes, not far from his own house and, though he had been brought up from boyhood by his grandfather, there were close bonds between him and his mother. By one of her small fields was a piece of rough ground and she offered him a piece of it for his chapel.

Already he had a name for it. Most of the Bible Christian chapels were given Biblical place-names and Billy's choice was not surprising. It would be Bethel, 'the house of the Lord.'

His 'core' at the mine was either morning, afternoon or night and such work as he intended to do must be done in his free time. At home with Joey were five children but he knew that she would readily care for them while he set to work on the foundations of the chapel. Indeed, if he had not been occupied in his mother's field he would hardly have been at home, for a good part of his time was already spent in a sort of wayside witnessing, walking from place to place in the knowledge that he would meet people with whom he could talk and share his faith. So, off to the field he went whenever he was free, clearing the hedge of the field and digging out foundation-ditches. He had no training as a builder but he knew he must at least begin by himself, whoever joined him later to help.

In fact, it was not help but opposition that he encountered.

'This little house is not good enough nor big enough,' he insisted in his class-meeting. 'We want a place to preach in, and the people a place to hear in.' Perhaps a few did, but most did not. 'It was not only the wicked that were against me. Most of the class turned against me and tried to turn the preachers against me.' Their objection seems to have been not to the building of a new chapel but to Billy's choice of site. The ditches were dug, nevertheless, and the foundation-stone set down.

It was a joyous day for Billy. There was a preacher to conduct worship, standing on the stone itself, and when the preaching ended Billy leapt on the stone.

'If this new chapel, which is to be called Bethel, stands for one hundred years, and one soul be converted in it every year, that will be one hundred souls, and one soul is worth more than all Cornwall', he cried. Suddenly his feet were tapping and he was leaping and dancing ecstatically on the

77

stone. 'Glory, glory, bless the Lord.' His voice echoed across the common and the fields. The neighbours in the cottages nearby shrugged and smiled cynically, There were enough chapels already for those that wanted them, and one man said so plainly.

'I shan't give you nothing for your chapel, Billy. You best go and beg somewhere else.'

In the view of some of Billy's supporters it was an unwise refusal. The man owned two horses which drew the 'whim' at the mine, drawing up the ore in a great bucket from the levels below. For no apparent reason one of them went lame while she was in the field, but to the neighbours the reason was plain. 'Didn't he say he wouldn't give nothing to the chapel?' They shook their heads in wisdom that came with hindsight, though few of them offered either money or help themselves. What followed seemed to be worse.

'The chapel was no use to that man, for he died soon after, and the Lord enabled me to build the chapel without his help.' Some of his friends did help, however, and when he had 'got some stone home to the place where the chapel was to be built, and the masons had put up some of the walls, I still had £1.15s. left.'

Now the argument broke out again. His fellow class-members insisted that it was in the wrong place and when he would not listen they went to the superintendent minister and complained that it should have been built at Twelveheads or Tippett's Stamps, nearby hamlets, instead. The superintendent told his colleague, in pastoral charge of the area, to sort matters out. He visited Billy before the preaching-service in the old house one weeknight.

'I told him *the Lord* had put it into my mind to build the chapel there and showed him what had been done already.'

Then, the preaching over in the little candle-lit room the preacher 'sorted things out'. 'Will you be willing to cast lots where the chapel should be built?' he asked.

Billy's opponents nodded and Billy agreed. 'I was willing,'

he recalled. 'I did not want to build the chapel there against the Lord's will. The preacher wrote three "lots", for Twelve-heads, Tippett's Stamps and Cross Lanes, the place where I had begun my chapel. When they drew lots the lot came out for Cross Lanes' where the chapel was begun.' Peace was restored. The critics said they would help and the preacher went home satisfied with the guidance and the promises that had been given.

'But telling about helping that night was all they did to help me. Next day one of them came and said to me that Cross Lanes still ought not to be the place, in spite of the lot-drawing.

'So I was as well off as I thought I should be!'

The work went ahead. 'The dear Lord helped me, for I had no money of my own.' Money came to pay the masons and the walls rose. Timber was bought for the roof, sawed up and set in place. But not enough of it. One principal beam was still missing – and there was no more wood and no money to buy it.

That morning a Wesleyan local preacher came looking for Billy and found him working at Bethel.

'What do you want a pound note for, Billy?' he demanded.

The little man stared at him. 'To buy timber to put a beam at that end of the roof there,' he answered.

The preacher shook his head in astonishment. 'Billy, I never knew such a thing in my life. While I was home praying this morning it kept on coming into my mind that I should come down and give you a pound note. So here it is!' He looked at the unfiinished building and went away, sharing something of Billy's joy as he did so.

Billy went on his way, too, leaping as he set off for Truro 'where I bought a principal (beam), put it on the chapel, and there it is to this day.' There was more to do yet, however, for the chapel needed thatching for the roof. He went round canvassing for help once more and got two pounds;

though he knew it would not go far he 'had faith to believe that Father would provide the rest'.

Suddenly tragedy stalked his home. The youngest of his small children was taken ill. Doctors were few and costly and, for the most part, local herbal folk remedies were all such families as his own could afford. They were effective in many cases, too, but where there were epidemics or serious illness the death-rate amongst children was very high.

Billy's child was so seriously ill that she seemed certain to die. 'The devil tempted me that she *would* die.' And if she did die?

He and Joey would grieve, but not for her. The reality of heaven as a place for little children, where Jesus would welcome his own as he did in his earthly life, was a fact they never doubted. But, for Billy, there was a much sharper conflict and another altercation with the devil.

'Satan tempted me that I had but two pounds and it would take seven pounds to cover (thatch) the chapel. But our little one would die and it would take one pound to bury her, and then I should have but one pound left. The devil tempted me very much on that point, for the dear Lord and me kept but one purse, and I paid any money that I earned at the mine to the chapel when I wanted it. So I had a right to take it.'

God's voice broke into the debate. 'It was applied to me, "Because thou hast built this chapel I will save thy child's life."

'And I said, "Where is this coming from?"

'And it was said to me, "I am the God of Abraham, Isaac and Jacob. Be nothing doubting. It is I, saith the Lord".'

He walked home from the unfinished chapel and, in his mind's eye, he could see the thatch on the roof as he turned away from it. In his heart there was a great peace – not yet the joy that made him dance and shout as he walked, but a deep and quiet confidence. He went into the living room of the cottage, where the child lay on a cot by the wall, hot and feverish. She whimpered as Billy put his hand on her forehead.

'The child will live,' he said quietly.

'Don't say so, Billy. The neighbours all say she will die. How can you say it?'

'The Lord has said she will live.'

There seemed no warrant for his faith. She was ill when he went to the mine, worse when he came home, and very ill during the night. Next morning showed no improvement and when he got home once more from his chapel-building she was still tossing restlessly.

'We knelt down to pray. The child was lying in the window-seat. We had for dinner what was very plentiful at that time, fish and potatoes. In my prayer I said, "Lord, thou hast said that the child shall live, but she has not eaten any food yet."

'She began to eat there and then. She is living now, and is the mother of ten children. So the Lord made the devil a liar once more!'

Faith was justified, and emboldened him to exercise it again. There was need of it in the next few weeks. With only two pounds – and he would need seven pounds before the roof was on – he borrowed a horse, rode up some twelve miles into the farming country, and asked a farmer if he had any reeds for sale.

'Yes,' said the farmer, 'at two pounds a hundred sheaves.'

'I told him to bring me three hundred sheaves as quick as he could, but I did not tell him that I only had two pounds. He brought down one hundred first and some "spears". I had three pounds when he came so I paid him for the reed and the spears and had a few shillings left. I asked the farmer to bring down the rest as soon as he could, but I didn't tell him I hadn't the money to pay for them. And it wasn't necessary that I should, for by the time the other sheaves were sent a friend gave me the money to pay for them.'

This was the story of Bethel. From foundation to opening-day it was a testing of faith, and just as Billy's faith never flagged so it was never disappointed. He needed a thatcher to lay the reeds, and ten shillings more than he possessed to pay for the work. On the highroad to the mines he shamed a miserly passer-by whom he knew well into giving it to him. He needed timber for doors and windows – and a nearby mine closed down and sold off its stock. For Billy there was a bargain in timber if he could find the money for it. The money came. But it still had to be fetched from the mine.

'One of our neighbours had a horse, but she would not draw. I asked him to lend her to me. He told me I might have her, but he warned me she would not draw a cart. But I took the mare, put her in the cart and brought the timber home.

'When I took back the mare I told him, "I never saw a better mare."

'He said, "I never saw such a thing in my life. She will not draw a cart for anybody!"'

Billy had an answer for him. 'That mare was working for a very strong company – Father, Son and Holy Ghost. Angels, men, devils – and horses! – must obey them!'

Bethel was built. The opposition, however, was not silenced. They assured him that there would be no preaching there. The place would not go on the 'plan'. They would see to it that the superintendent minister did not appoint any preachers to it. Billy locked the door and took the key home with him. As he hung it up on a nail behind the door he offered it to God. 'Lord, the chapel is built and there is the key. I have done what thou didst tell me to do.'

Faith was proved once again. The superintendent 'that very day' not only 'put it on the plan' but appointed preachers more often than Billy could have wished. 'We had preaching there every Sunday, afternoon and evening, and class meeting in the morning. The Lord soon revived his work and we gathered a great many members.' In time the little chapel proved far too small and a new one had to be built, leaving the old one for use as Sunday-school and meeting place.

Much later Billy looked back on it all. 'No wonder the devil was so against me while I was building the old Bethel, and put his servants to hinder me, for I have seen at one time fifty down on their knees asking for mercy, and mercy they had.'

Not far from Billy's home by Twelveheads is Kerley Downs, and it was here that he built the second of his three chapels. It was to have 'three windows, one on the one side, two on the other. The old devil, who does not like chapels, put his servants by way of reproach to call our chapel "Three-Eyes".' For five generations or so the mocking nickname has been used with affection by Methodists all over Cornwall, and it quickly became one of the most familiar and widely-known landmarks of the Billy Bray country. Not least was this so because one of his best-loved stories was attached to it.

It should perhaps be emphasised that though Billy was, for a while, a committed chapel-builder he was no separatist or schismatic. He did not then, or ever, seek to attract followers to himself. While he repelled some by his eccentricities, as they saw his unconventional behaviour in and out of the pulpit, he attracted far more, so that by the mid-point of his preaching career the very announcement of his name would ensure a full and overflowing chapel. Yet he never capitalised on this in any way. He was 'the Lord's servant', and no more than that. He had joined the Bible Christians at Hicks Mill immediately after his conversion and remained a 'Bryanite' all his life.

If these buildings were known, inevitably since he did so much of the money-raising and the actual building of them, as 'Billy Bray's chapels', he held no vested interest in them. The chapels were part of the Bible Christian circuit, observed the discipline of that Church and relied on its ministers for oversight and direction. If they also relied to an almost overwhelming extent on local lay leadership and lay preachers this was exactly the same as the whole of rural Methodism, whatever its denomination.

Today, the visitor to Cornwall finds it over-churched to an unusual degree. Every little village has a couple of Methodist chapels, and every hamlet at least one. Many are now closed, but that they should ever have been opened at all – and that Billy should have thought of adding to them – may well seem nonsensical. In fact, from Wesley's day through to the middle of the last century, Cornwall was heavily populated and highly industrialised throughout the mining areas – and mining was not confined to west Cornwall where so many of the old engine-houses now stand gauntly pointing their shattering chimney stack to the sky. Tin and copper were mined all over Cornwall, except in the central moorlands, though the concentration was in the west. Billy's estimate of the average miner as 'wicked and godless' may well have been an overstatement by a man who saw everything in 'black and white', but all the various branches of Methodism – Wesleyan, Primitive and Bible Christian – saw the thousands of unchurched men and women as a challenge. They must witness everywhere, and chapels were the base from which they worked and the 'home' in which new Christians were nurtured in worship and class-meeting.

If there was a hamlet or a village full of the unconverted *that* was a place where a chapel was needed.

So Billy went to speak to the class-meeting which gathered in a small cottage at Kerley Downs. ''Tis too small for our needs, Mr Bray,' they said. 'If twenty people crowd in for the preaching on Sunday there isn't room for another soul.'

Billy began to hear the whisper of the Lord.

'If you build a chapel at Cross Lanes why couldn't you

build one here at Kerley Downs? 'Tis no more than a mile from your own home.'

'Have you got any money towards it?' asked Billy.

'Yes, some. We made a collection to buy the ground and 'twas promised to us. But then 'twas sold to a man who offered a higher price for it.'

Then a local farmer met one of the class. 'Where is the money you collected for the chapel? You haven't begun to build it yet.' When the story was told he made an offer. 'If you have a mind to build a chapel you may have some ground of me.'

Billy found himself immediately involved in the project.

'I told the minister we could have a spot for a chapel, and if he did not call a meeting to appoint trustees I should begin the building myself. So he appointed a day, and got trustees – but all that promised to help me left me to myself. So my little son and me went to work, and got some stone. The good friend who gave us the land lent me his horse and cart, and we soon had the masons to work.'

He was distressed that none of those who had apparently been so anxious to have a chapel in their midst did anything to help build it, and once more the devil took a hand – but only briefly.

'When our chapel was up to about the door-head the devil said to me, "They are all gone and left you, and the chapel. I would go and leave the place, too."'

'Then I said, "Devil, doesn't thee know me better than that? By the Lord's help I will have the chapel up, or lose my skin on the down." So the devil said no more to me on that subject!'

His pictorial language shrouds the very real depressions that must have attacked the little miner time after time. He strove against opposition, which he could fight, and more often against inertia and irresponsibility amongst his supporters which was more difficult to combat. There was never more than enough money for immediate needs, and often not even that. Physically he must often have been completely exhausted, as he gave every spare minute from the mine either to working on the chapels or to collecting money for them. And poverty still dogged his home, for he gave away more than he could afford, and certainly what his wife Joey often needed for the family budget.

But at last the chapel was 'up' and the roof thatched. Where, however, was the pulpit to come from? At last, looking round some furniture at an auction sale, he saw an old three-cornered cupboard. It was the very thing. He nudged his neighbour. 'I do want it for a pulpit up to Kerley Downs. I can cut a slit down the back, strengthen the middle, put a reading-board up in front, clap a pair of steps behind – and the preacher will have a handsome pulpit.'

'You're Billy Bray, aren't 'ee?'

'Yes,' he acknowledged. 'How much do 'ee think the cupboard will fetch?'

'About six shillings, I should think. I'll give 'ee six shillings to buy it.'

Billy was gleeful, and as soon as the cupboard was put up he shouted to the auctioneer. 'Here, mister. Here's six shillings for it. I do want it for a pulpit.'

In the roar of laughter the auctioneer caught a bid from another part of the room. He raised his gavel and smacked the table. 'Sold for seven shillings.'

Billy was dumbfounded. 'No, mister. Not seven. Six. Here's the money.' He shrugged ruefully. 'If Father don't want me to have it, that must be right.' He looked round to give the money back to his friendly neighbour but the man had gone. 'Then I'll be gone, too, and have a word with Father.' He set off for Kerley Downs and the pulpitless chapel. His praying finished, he came out in time to see the cupboard coming up the hill on a cart and, out of curiosity, followed to see where it was going. Stopping outside a house the men heaved the cupboard off the cart and up to the door. "'Twill never go in!' muttered Billy as they tried to push it, and then drag it, inside. And, indeed, though they tried it forwards and backwards, endways and sideways, it was an inch or two too big for the door.

Billy went up the path. 'Seven shillings spent for nothin',' growled the purchaser to his helpers. 'All I can do is scat (break) it up for firewood!'

'You could do better than that,' said Billy, at his elbow. 'If I give 'ee six shillings for it will 'ee carry it down to my little chapel for me?'

So the three-cornered cupboard became the pulpit at Kerley Downs and Billy danced for joy. 'Bless the Lord,' he shouted as he leapt round the room. 'Father knew I couldn't carry it up here myself, even if I did buy it, so he've got someone to carry it up for me, too. Praise his name!' he cried as he leapt again.

Once more as the opening day came he repeated what he had said at Cross Lanes. 'If one soul were converted every year for a hundred years, that would be a hundred souls, and I should be rich in heaven.' But the opening service gave no promise, at least to Billy. 'We had preaching, but the preacher (minister) was a wise man, and a dead man. It was a very dead time with preacher and people. He had a great deal of "grammar" but very little of "Father".

'The second Sunday after the chapel was opened I was "planned" there. I said to the people, "You know I did not work here about this chapel in order to fill my own pocket, but for the good of the neighbours, and the good of souls. And souls I must have, and souls I will have."'

This was the kind of preaching they had waited for. Witty and earnest, this man who spoke their own tongue and knew their own lives, exhorted, warned, shouted and pleaded with them.

'The Lord blessed us in a wonderful manner. Two women cried for mercy, and I said, "The chapel is paid for already."

'The dear Lord went to work there and the membership went up from fifteen to thirty.

'You see how good the dear Lord is to me! I asked for one soul a year and he gave me fifteen in the first year!'

9

'Honey in a Ladle'

The Bible Christians, in those early years, were still a small denomination whose members were rural and poor people. They had little money and small help from outside their own community. But what they lacked in material resources they more than made up in faith. From experience, they added another 'credo' to their simple creed.

'I believe the Lord will provide.'

That he did so is beyond question – and what was true for the Church as a whole was proved in the lives of its members and leaders. Though he was never a 'leader' even in his local circuits and largely unknown for most of his life beyond his own county, Billy Bray's life-story, when it was written by F. W. Bourne, must have struck a familiar chord throughout the whole Bible Christian Connexion. If ever the Lord provided for those who served him faithfully, he did so beyond doubt for Billy. It was proved in his personal life, despite the frustrations his wife Joey suffered because of his uncalculating generosity. It was proved in his building of Bethel and Kerley Downs chapels, and proved again in the building of Great Deliverance at Carharrack.

Carharrack, now a large village straggling from the slopes of Carn Marth down the edge of the desolate but once busy area of United Mines was in the parish of Gwennap, though the 'church-town' lay some little distance away. It was here at Carharrack that the 'tinners' had gathered outside John Wesley's lodging on his first visit to Cornwall and roused him with their singing before the drawn broke. The parish church probably had comparatively little effect on the lives of the miners, though the Wesleyans were well established in the area. It is notable that, in a survey of Cornish Bible Christian circuits, it was shown that nearly half their members had been gained in almost equal proportions from the Wesleyans and the Anglican Church. The presence of Wesleyan and Anglican places of worship did not, however, deter Billy when he 'heard the word of the Lord'.

'The Lord led me to build another chapel' at Carharrack and 'put it into the heart of a gentleman to grant me a piece of land.'

The early days were full of 'the Lord's provision'.

'The Lord put into my heart to go down by the railway' (used for carrying ore in small trucks) 'to raise stone. Someone had been there before and their quarry was poor.'

The passers-by made their opinion plain. ''Tis no use quarryin' there, Billy my son. There isn't nothin' there at all. You can see that by lookin' at it!' But had not God sent him to the 'tramway'?

'The others had worked to the east and the west', he records, 'and left a piece of ground untouched in the middle. We went to work on this place and the good Lord helped me, as he said. Some wondered at how much stone we got out. But' (as with the mare that would not 'draw') 'I was working for a strong company, Father, Son and Holy Ghost, and that company will never break!'

But building costs money, and masons' wages must be paid. Billy had none, or only enough to go to the coffee-shop by the mine and spend sixpence on his breakfast and then away to the 'tramline' to raise stone. He had 'no bank but the bank of heaven. But, thanks be to God, that is a *strong* bank, and I often had to go there in faith.' It was, however, very practical faith. Money from *this* bank really had to be drawn. With the building rising above its foundations and the stone hewn from the quarry he set out to find where he could get it, sure that God would provide it if he acted under his guidance.

'I went round collecting.'

It sounds simpler than it was. His eye was on the south and the west – Camborne, Helston, St Just near Land's End, and St Ives. Of Camborne he says nothing, except that 'the friends were very kind to me', though such gifts as he received must usually have been small, coming as they did from people who themselves had little. Helston, on the other hand, rates a page or so in his record. 'There lived a miser who was said to be worth a great deal of money who was never known to give anything to any object.' He retorted that he could not afford anything when Billy asked him for help.

'I am begging for the Lord's house,' said Billy, 'and if you do not give me something the Lord may take you away from your money, or your money away from you!' He went on to assure him that his gold was the Lord's property, not his.

'Go round the town and see what you can get, and come back and see me by and by.'

Billy goes on with some vivid description. 'I said to him, "No, you've got money and I must have some *now*." I talked to him about what the Lord did with greedy people. Then he wiped his mouth, put his hand in his pocket four or five times, and talked away. At last he took out two shillings and sixpence and gave me. I don't think Satan let him sleep that night because the dear Lord had let me take half-a-crown from his god.'

'It was the greatest miracle ever performed in Helston,' said some of the friends.

For Billy, without his own horse-and-trap, the only way to reach either Camborne or Helston, or anywhere else for for that matter, was by walking. Sundays he retained as 'the

Lord's day', wherever he might be working, but in order to reach St Just, where he was planned to preach one Sunday, it meant an early start and a long walk over poor roads and poorer tracks, for St Just was a twenty-five mile walk. Most preaching-services seem to have been in the afternoons on Sunday, with the morning given over to the class-meetings, but even so he would have set out before dawn crept over the lip of Carn Marth. When he had 'done his work' at St Just, and collected what he could, he went on to St Ives.

The year was 1838, fifteen years after his conversion and his first appearance on the Bible Christian 'plan', and he had already become widely known. A 'popular preacher', he was often invited to conduct special services and 'revival meetings' amongst the Wesleyan Methodists as well as his own Bible Christians.

St Ives, now amongst the most popular resorts in Britain, was then two villages – Down-long, the fishing village by the harbour and round the base of the 'island', and Stennack, the mining village a few hundred yards away. It was, even in Billy's estimation, 'a small place', where there was real enmity between minders and fishermen, and where a bad fishing season could bring the fishing village, Downlong, near to starvation.

Billy was met when he arrived by a friend, Mr Bryant. 'He told me I had come at a very poor time, for there was very little fish caught that year, and some of the people were almost wanting bread.'

'It was poor times with Peter,' said Billy, 'when the Lord told him to let down his net on the other side of the ship,' but to Mr Bryant the lake of Galilee and the rocky coast lashed by the Atlantic were very different places. He did not say so, but it would need a miracle greater than the touching of a miser's heart in Helston to keep the fisherfolk from hunger.

'We went up to the Wesleyan chapel. There were a great

many lively souls and we had a good meeting. We prayed to
the Lord to send some fish. After the meeting we went to the
coffee-house to get some refreshment and then went back to
the meeting, and continued it till midnight, keeping on praying to the Lord to send in the fish . . .

'And, as we came out of the meeting to go to our lodging,
there were the poor, dear women with the pilchards on their
plates, and the fish shining in the moonlight. The women
were smiling, the moon was smiling, and we were smiling,
and no wonder for the dear Lord put bread on many
shelves that night and blessed many families.'

The harbour was a riot of noise, with men shouting
urgently as the pilchards were heaved out onto the quayside,
glistening in heaps on the wet slabs. Many of the boats,
racing out to sea when the 'huer' whose task it was to keep
watch for the dark shoals under the water had shouted his
sighting-cry of 'Heva! Heva!', had taken ten thousand fish
that night, and others had done better and taken twenty
thousand. Long before midnight, while the meeting was still
praying for fish, the fish were already in the boats – and
Billy would make something of that parable. 'He answers us
before we call!' Now, working through the night, the
women gutted the fish, hundred after hundred, swiftly and
expertly flinging the guts away to be guzzled by thousands of
gulls all along the harbour front. As they were opened and
piled up the fish were as quickly shovelled into barrels and
covered with salt. By the next day there were eight thousand
casks of pilchards salted away.

But fish were still bounding in the water, and Billy suddenly saw the Lord's purpose in his coming to St Ives.
'Some of the fishermen said to me, "Now you shall have
some money for your chapel. If you get a boat and come out
with us we will give you some fish." A carpenter, a friend of
mine, a bit used to the sea, got a boat and rowed me to the
place where the fish were. They looked pretty, shining and

dancing about in the water, and the fishermen dipped up the fish and threw them into our boat. When we came to land the carpenter sold the fish and I took the money which amounted to £6.15s.'

'A druggist, also, promised me the profits on his week's taking, and that brought me two guineas more.

'Altogether I took away from St Ives seventeen pounds towards the chapel.'

The chapel began to rise, but what about the roof, wondered Billy. It was then that a generous local man, whom he refers to as 'Mr T.' came to him. St Ives was much in Billy's mind when the 'gentleman' asked what he was building. 'I'm going to build a fishing-net,' Billy told him, 'to catch the fine fish that are out there in the shoals round Carharrack.'

'I'll come and look at it,' said his questioner, and when they arrived at Carharrack he expressed his astonishment at so large a building. 'Well,' said Billy, 'the shoals round here are big, too!'

'This sort of fishing net needs a roof, I suppose?' Billy nodded. 'Bless the Lord, my Father deserves a large house, don't he?'

Mr T. smiled at his enthusiasm. 'Then I will give you a large roof, Mr Bray. You'll want timber and slate, I suppose? Then come down to my store and you shall have all you need.'

It was one of Billy's joys that, when Great Deliverance chapel was built and opened, Mr T. was to become a staunch member of it and a valuable leader. And Great Deliverance itself was to be scene of 'revivals' and, for more than a century, the centre of vigorous fellowship and lively worship. To Billy himself, the building of it was a series of marvellous reassurances that 'the Lord would provide'.

The faith that sustained him in his chapel-building was no greater than the dependence on God which was the mark of his daily life. He had great need of it. What he called 'trials' were an everyday experience. He had a mentally-ill sister who caused him, and the rest of the family, great distress. He had five children whose size and appetites grew with every year that passed, though his wages never rose in proportion to their needs. Indeed, unemployment is no new phenomenon in the mining industry and, as the hopes of some company of 'mining adventurers' faded when the shaft did not produce tin or copper quickly or easily enough to provide quick profits, they would close it down rather than risk further losses and all who had worked at that particular mine were out of a job. Billy had periods when he was out of work more often than he was employed. And even when he was at work the money was poor, though as time went by he had more stable periods and better posts as a 'sub-captain' or something of the kind.

It was in one of the darker times that he came home from the mine with no money. This time he had not given it away to someone whom he thought to be in greater poverty than himself. The counting-house clerk had simply told the men that there was nothing to pay them with. Next week, no doubt, there would be more ore, a new strike in another and lower level, wages restored again, but this week. . . The clerk sent them away grumbling but impotent.

Joey grumbled, too. ''Tis all your own fault, Billy. Even when you've got money in your hand you do give it away. What shall us do now, with not a loaf of bread in the cupboard?'

She had hardly finished speaking and banged away angrily when there was a knock at the door.

'I heard you got no money this week, Mr Bray,' said the visitor, and handed him a basket. It held everything the family needed, and as the 'good Samaritan' went back down the little path to the rickety gate he heard Billy's voice. Rapturously if without much musical skill he was singing as loudly as he could.

'Not fearing or doubting,
    With Christ on my side,
I hope to die shouting
    The Lord will provide.'

And as he walked away from the cottage he could hear Billy calling out. 'Didn't I tell 'ee, Joey? Glory and praise the Lord!'

To Billy, 'Father' would never forget.

To many people such faith might appear simplistic, the extension of half-a-dozen instances of apparent answers to prayer, in themselves no more than coincidence, which an eccentric and unrealistic village miner had built into a total philosophy of life. True, he suffered reverses, deprivation and occasions when his prayers were not immediately answered in an obvious and positive way. But it is equally notable that his journal, his sermons and the memories of other people about him were full of constant and repetitive instances in which his needs were met, for himself, his family, his chapels and the people he tried to help.

'Great Deliverance' was not merely the name of a chapel he built, it was the recurring theme of his experience.

The most obvious examples are the simplest.

Cornish roads in the winter were often little more than stony tracks running with rain and mine-water, ankle deep in thick mud. Coming home one night from a preaching appointment Billy went worse than ankle deep. Dragging his feet out of the morass he tore the whole of the thin sole off his boot. Ruefully, as he recalled, he stood with his broken boot in his hand, and showed it heavenwards. 'I've wore these boots out in thy cause, Father, and I've no money to buy new ones.' He thrust his foot into the broken boot and hobbled homewards, to go to work in the other pair he used for the mine.

'I want you to come with me to Truro,' said a friend the next week. And, once there, he took Billy to a boot-and-shoe shop for new boots and then, for good measure, fitted him out with some extra clothing. 'If you won't buy nothing for yourself, my son, someone had better do it for 'ee!'

The plain fact behind that story, and others, is that this simple man was so beloved for what he was and did that the story of a predicament like boots torn to pieces in the mud was likely to bring someone to his aid. But, since not even Billy expected new boots to fall from the skies, this was as much an answer to prayer as any other.

The same may well be true of the lost frock. It was a story often told.

'I walked into Truro to buy a frock for my little maid (child) and, coming homelong, I felt so full of happiness that I caught up my heels a bit every now and again and danced for joy.

'When I got home Joey said, "What have 'ee done with the frock?"

'"'Tis in the basket."

'"No such thing. There's nothing there at all."

'So then I knew what must have happened and I told her.

'"Glory to God, I must have danced the frock out of the basket on the way home!"

Billy was not a man to keep so gloriously funny a story to himself, and the next morning, Sunday, he shared it in his class-meeting. He was certainly unworldly enough to do so without any ulterior intention, but when he got home he was dancing again, and leaped about the kitchen for joy. His friends had given him enough money to buy another frock. But that was not the end of the story.

'Two or three days afterwards someone picked up the frock and brought it home to me. So the little maid had two frocks for the price of one. Glory! Glory! Glory!'

There were less obvious, or as some critics would say, contrived answers to his prayers. One of them he told himself and, while it would have an immediate understanding response from a congregation of miners, it also illustrated one of his most notable qualities, his sheer persistence. At the time he was a 'captain-dresser' – a foreman in charge of sorting and processing the tin and copper ore brought up from the mine. He took on half-a-dozen boys and girls to work on it. The system meant that he had to agree their wages, and pay them out of what he himself was paid for the ore on the 'setting-day' at the end of the month. On this occasion, having put in his bid for the particular piece of work, the ore which came up from the level seemed unbelievably poor. Those who looked at it from time to time assured him that it was worthless.

'That means there won't be nothing for *me* at the end of the month, and there won't be nothing for these boys and girls, neether. I do know what the people will say. "There's that old Billy Bray, that old Bryanite, that old rogue – he've cheated the boys and maidens out of their wages."

'But whilst I was praying the Lord said to me, "I will bring thee through," And I said, "I believe it, Lord. If thou tell me thou'lt bring me through, I believe it. And now I don't care what the old devil says."

'And every time they came past and said to me that it wasn't worth nothing I told them. "I don't care whether the stuff is worth anything or not, but the Lord have told me he will bring me through and he will."

'And do 'ee think the Lord failed me after that? No! When the ore was sampled at the end of the month it was better than I had believed or anyone else had believed. 'Twas good enough to pay me *my* wages, and the wages for the boys and the maidens, and to leave me £5 over and over it all for myself! Glory! Praise the Lord! Bless his name!'

Despite these stories there was nothing introverted about Billy's religion. If he cared about people's souls and offered them the joys of heaven for those who believed, he did not see this as a doctrine that should reconcile them to misery below. Knowing the anguish of poverty and hunger himself he found it difficult to pass by the cottages of other people in the same situation without trying to help. He gave away more than he should out of his own pocket, and when his own money was exhausted, he begged from other people. Throughout west Cornwall there were small Quaker communities – one of the best-known Quaker meeting-houses is at Come-to-Good, at Feock, only a few miles from Billy's home – and these people were often better-off than most and almost invariably generous. They appear again and again as helpers in Billy's own story and on many occasions he went to them so that he could help his poorer neighbours. Not only so, but he was quite prepared to go to the 'gentry' for the same reason.

On one occasion when he was begging for money to help someone in need he was about to march up to the front door when his companion tugged at his sleeve to halt him and urged him to go round to the back.

'They're gentry, Billy. Thee can't go hammerin' on the front door!'

'Why not?' responded Billy. 'I'm the King's son, and I'm on the King's business.'

Inside he would treat them with deference and explain his mission, but that did not prevent him being himself. On one occasion the gentleman gave him a sovereign and the lady some spare clothes and asked him to take tea with them. Ready to leave Billy turned round and knelt to pray for them, and for the poor they had helped. God, to Billy, was no respecter of persons, and was certainly as likely to bless the generous rich as the poor they helped.

It was his own generosity that irked his wife Joey, however.

'We shall be brought to the Union (workhouse) if you do go on like this, Billy!' she said in exasperation. But that thought did not stop him. The Lord would never see *him* brought to the Union, or his family.

'At one time,' he recounted, 'I had been at work the whole of the month but had no wages to take home when pay-day came. We had no bread in the house so Joey told me to go and see the Captain to let me have a few shillings. I did what she said and he let me have ten shillings. On my way home I called to see a family, but I found they were worse off than I was myself. We had no bread, but we did have bacon and potatoes, and they had neither. So I gave them five shillings and went off towards home. Then I called in to see another family and found they were worse off still. So I gave them the other five shillings and went home.

'"Have 'ee seen the captain?" Joey asked.

'"Yes."

'"Did he give 'ee any money?"

'"Yes."

'"Well, where is it??"

'So I told her what I'd done. "I gave it away," and I told her who to.

'Joey said, "I never seen the fellow to 'ee in all my life. You *will* have us in the Union, whatever you say."

'But I told her, "The Lord isn't going to stay in *my* debt for very long, you can be sure."

'Well, Joey was some miserable after that, but two or three days afterwards when I come home from the mine she was all smiles instead.

'"What have happened to 'ee?"

"Mrs So-and-so have been here."

'"Oh?"

'"She left me a sovereign."

'"Now, didn't I tell 'ee the Lord wouldn't stay in my debt? The bank of faith is the best bank in the world. Father have not only paid me back the half-sovereign I gave away, but he've given me half-a-sovereign interest as well!"'

For a careful woman like Joey, with five children to clothe and feed, living with a man like Billy may have been and education in faith, but it could be a trial of faith as well, and it often was.

For Billy, on the other hand, faith seemed to rise triumphantly above the immediate realities of poverty and hunger. A more careful reading of his words, however, is revealing. Faith only 'seemed' easy and natural to his hearers when he spoke about it. Behind his bright wit and the memorably-told personal anecdotes was another story, a tale of the struggle to hold fast to faith. This was by no means as easy as he made it sound, and 'doubt' was his constant enemy.

If the greatest of the saints had their 'dark nights of the soul' it is unlikely that such a man as Billy Bray went walking on the mountain-tops all his life. Today we are accustomed to find people's doubts expressed in philosophical terms. In our own minds we have to face doubts about God's reality, or his love or power over events, and we try to argue our way through to peace again either in our thinking or in consultation with other people. Billy's struggle with doubt he dramatised and personalised as 'conversation-pieces' with the devil. He knew the ebb and flow of feeling that is part of any emotional experience, and he regarded the times when he was 'down' as 'the devil trying to rob him of joy', but his sharpest conflicts were undoubtedly related to his everyday life. Why was it not easier to get money and personal support for his chapels as he tried 'to do the Lord's will' by building them? Why was there opposition to what, for him, was manifestly the Lord's way of doing things? Why, perversely, did the wicked flourish and the righteous suffer hunger? Why – though he did not often admit to putting it this way – did *he* suffer when he did everything he could and gave everything he had to further God's kingdom in his own bit of Cornwall?

The last of these doubts he translates into vivid terms in one sermon, and the setting of the conflict is his own potato-patch.

'Friends, last week I was diggin' up my 'taters. It was a wisht (miserable) crop, sure 'nough. There was hardly a sound one in the whole lot of them. And while I was digging the devil come to me, and he says, "Billy, do you think your Father do love 'ee?" An' I said, "I reckon he do." "Well, I don't," says the old tempter directly. If I'd thought about it I shouldn't have listened to 'un for half a minute for his opinions bain't worth the least bit of notice. But he went on quick. "I don't, and I'll tell 'ee for why. If your Father loved you, Billy Bray, he'd give 'ee a handsome yield of 'taters – so much as ever you do want, and ever so many of them, and everyone of them as big as your hand. For it bain't no trouble for your Father to do anything, and he could just as easy give you plenty as not. And if he loved you he would do, too!"

'Of course, I wasn't goin' to let him to talk of my Father like that, so I turned round upon 'un. "And who may you be, coming and talkin' to me like that? If I bain't mistaken I know who *you* are and I know my Father, too. And to think of *you* coming and sayin' he don't love me! Why, I got your written character home to my house – and it do say you're a liar from the beginnin'! Let me tell 'ee that I used to have a personal acquaintance with you some time since. I served you as faithfully as any wretch could do. And what did you give me? All you ever gave me was rags to my back, an' a wretched home, and an achin' head, and the fear of hell-fire to come – and no 'taters at all! An' here's my dear Father in Heaven – what have *he* given me? He's given me a clean heart, and a soul full of joy, and a suit of white as will never wear out. And he says he'll make a king of me before he've done and take home to his palace to live with him for ever and ever. And to think that you dare come up here and talk to me like that!"

'Bless 'ee, my dear friends, he went off in a minute like as if he'd been shot!'

It is easy to realise that this was no single conflict with doubt, and that the battle was not always so easily won.

Yet, in the end, joy always broke through. The tougher the

trial the more rapturous, for this ecstatic little man, was the triumph.

Traditions about folk-heroes tend to make some events more colourful than they actually were, and 'the bung hole in the barrel' is a case of that kind. It was a common tradition in Cornwall that Billy was standing on a barrel in the market-place at Falmouth, or Truro, or Redruth – the place varied – and was jeered for his wild antics in the name of religion. In this story Billy replied, 'If I danced my way through the barrel I would shout "Hallelujah" through the bung-hole!' The story always ended with Billy capering more wildly than ever, the end of the cask collapsing and the little man disappearing out of sight while his loud voice still went on, as he had promised, 'shouting Hallelujah through the bung-hole'.

The story seems merely to be an improvisation on one of his more familiar retorts to some who were criticising him for his 'wild ways'.

'If they were to put me in a barrel I would shout out "Glory!" through the bung-hole.' Whether it actually happened or not, that he would have done so there is little doubt. He was at times uncontrollable and his joy uncontainable – and that in spite of the doubts and trials which were his travelling companions.

Less familiar than the barrel story is another which sums up exactly how he looked at life.

It was later in his life, when he had moved for some years from the St Day and Twelveheads area to St Neots near Bodmin. The Primitive Methodist minister found Billy at a love-feast in the 'Prim's 'chapel at St Blazey, an occasion when testimonies flowed freely after a symbolic 'meal' of bread and water. The testimonies were hardly exhilarating, and those who spoke seemed to have had more than their fair share of trials and disappointments.

Then Billy rose in his place. His face was smiling and as

he got to his feet he was clapping his hands in excitement.

'Listen, my dear friends,' he cried. 'All my life I've had to take vinegar and honey. But, praise the Lord, I've had to take the vinegar with a spoon – but he's given the honey with a ladle!'

10

The Charismatic Community

One of the Bible Christian ministers, appointed to the St
Austell circuit in mid-Cornwall, heard Billy preach at the
anniversary service at Tywardreath Highway chapel. It was
an occasion he never forgot. The chapel was crowded to the
doors, including the aisle between the seats, the steps of the
pulpit and the entrance itself where the congregation spilled
out onto the road. It was not possible, he thought, for the
preacher to get to the pulpit. Then, at the door, there was a
shout.

'Bless the Lord! Little Billy is come again to Highway!'

It was impossible to mistake the tone and the words.
Billy was announcing himself, as so often, in the third person. The congregation turned as well as it could to see Billy,
dressed in his dark suit and white tie, making his way down
the passage that had somehow opened for him. There was
no room to dance this time, but the smile that transformed
his dark and serious face into gaiety and the ejaculations
that burst out from him as he moved through the church
showed that he would have done if the space had been
there. He was less restrained when he reached the pulpit
and, before he finally announced the hymn, he was leaping
and shouting out praise that he was with his friends once
more.

'Oh for a thousand tongues to sing
My great Redeemer's praise.'

Before the 'pitcher' could raise the first, correct note for the congregation to follow Billy was shouting again. 'That's nine hundred and ninety-nine more than I've got.' And, as the man at the front of the chapel pitched the first clear note, Billy was talking once more, almost to himself. 'And if I did have nine hundred and ninety-nine more than I have now I would be singing and shouting "Glory!" with every one of them!'

That evening Mr Gilbert, the minister, spent an hour or two with Billy.

'I saw your mother down at Twelveheads.'

'Did 'ee now! And how was the dear soul?'

'She's an old woman, Billy. And you know she's blind. But we had a blessed time of prayer together.'

'Happy, was she?'

'Yes. Very happy. While I was praying with her she jumped up and danced round the house. She was shouting praises just as you do.'

'Dancin', was she?' said Billy, his voice lifting suddenly. A wave of excitement swept through him and he, too, jumped to his feet and began to leap round the room. Mr Gilbert looked at him. There was no pattern, no special rhythm to his jumping amongst the furniture. It was an uncontrollable ecstasy. 'Dear old soul! I'm glad to hear she danced! Bless the Lord! Why shouldn't I dance as well as King David? When you do love the Lord you can't keep your feet still!'

It might seem that his 'dancing' was part of an inherited and explosive nervous tension. But that would be the wrong explanation, as a comment from another source shows very well.

The co-founder of the Primitive Methodist Church, which began in the Midlands and the Potteries at about the same time as the Bible Christians in the West Country, was visiting Cornwall in 1825. William Clowes and Hugh Bourne had been expelled from the Wesleyan Methodists for disregarding its discipline and, against the will of their superintendent ministers, holding 'camp meetings'. Clowes was therefore not unaccustomed to a measure of emotion and the reality both of conversion and the joy it brought. He attended some of the Bible Christian services and meetings in the Redruth area but his comment is significant. Invited to preach in a house in Twelveheads, Billy Bray's own hamlet, he was greatly affronted. 'Several of Mr O'Bryan's people who were present in the worship began to laugh and dance. I was grieved at their conduct for many people, who had come to hear preaching, were disappointed by witnessing their noise and actions.'

If a radical and vigorous man like William Clowes was critical of the Bible Christian's behaviour it is not surprising that more formal people were much more upset by it, and that the 'outsiders' found it a source of easy ridicule. But, at least, Clowes' comment indicates that others besides Billy had the same extrovert ways of expressing themselves – even if, perhaps, Billy and some of his Twelveheads friends were in the middle of that particular diversion.

The plain fact is that, almost from the beginning, the Bible Christians were a charismatic community, expressing their faith, fellowship and fervour with typical freedom and sometimes apparent abandon. They would seem to have talked about Jesus more than they talked about the Holy Spirit, perhaps, and there is no clear evidence of the use of glossolalia, or 'tongues' but their uninhibited joy, their strong sense of belonging together and much of their personal discipline has a charismatic mark though none of them had ever heard the word. In particular this appears to have been true of their worship, their meetings and their pressure towards conversion and a complete change of life.

The emphasis on the Spirit was there, nevertheless, and

not least in some of Billy Bray's own records. He visited an old lady of eighty, for instance, who 'knew as much about the dear Lord as I could tell her'. Every word she spoke was sweet to his ears. 'Like Saul and Barnabas, she was filled with the Holy Ghost – and Satan can do nothing by they who are filled by him!'

Though public worship almost merged into 'after-meetings' there was a fairly clear distinction between the order (if not always the orderliness) of worship and the apparent disorder that followed as freedom was given to all who were present. Billy Bray was not the only preacher to 'shout his way to the pulpit', or to punctuate his sermons, and even the hymns and scripture, with 'Glory' and 'Praise the Lord'. Indeed, both he and most of the preachers would have felt that the life had gone out of worship if there had not been a running response of 'Hallelujah!' and 'Amen!' Those places in which this constant response was absent were, in Bible Christian terminology, regarded as 'dead'. A preacher 'might as well preach to the haystacks in the field' and would have felt just as much at home, and his own reaction to such a lack of lively reinforcement of his own words would either be to 'dry up' or to redouble his efforts with more eloquent gestures and thumpings of the pulpit and louder accusations against the sin of indifference.

Worship included hymns – though not many, as a rule, for hymn-books were costly and scarce and each hymn had to be 'lined out'. The preacher would read two lines and they would be sung under the leading of a member of the congregation before the next two or three were 'lined out'. At the same time, of course, many of them would be well-known and sung without this sort of aid, and the most familiar would be sung again and again. The service might well last an hour and a half, and the sermon (much of it re-iterated and some of it no doubt tedious, for not all had the ability and wit of Billy or the background of the greater leaders of the Church) was likely to last at least three-quarters of an hour. The prayer, full of scripture quotations, relevant and irrelevant, might well be twenty minutes long. This, indeed, was very much the pattern in most of the country chapels of Cornwall, in all the branches of Methodism, until well into the present century, and lay preachers tended to 'last' longer than the ordained ministers.

Services of worship were usually held in the afternoon and /or the evening and the 'class-meetings' in the morning. At, the beginning, even in the towns, and certainly in the fairly primitive buildings in the country the only light was from candles or 'rushes' – wicks dipped in oil and kept in a base of oil. Only later did gas-lighting become fairly general and even then it was for most of the century non-existent in the country chapels.

Candles, in any case, had an occasional use which gas could not have provided. Thomas Tregaskis, whom Billy knew well as a fellow-member of Hicks Mill chapel and who was to become a well-known local preacher, found them very much suited to his purpose. Following the early Bible Christian habit of denouncing the frippery of dress which betokened unspirituality of heart, Tregaskis would pick up some of the more flimsy items of ladies' costume which their owners threw away under his direction and burn them over the pulpit candles!

It was when the service was over and the 'after-meeting' began that 'liberty' took hold of the congregation. Thomas Shaw, in his brief history of *The Bible Christians* refers to Michaelstow where a society began in 1818 and a villager complained that he could not sleep on Sunday because of the chorusing at an early hour. 'This was the place,' comments Shaw, at which some of the members looked suspiciously at Samuel Thorne (one of the early leaders of the Church) because it had been rumoured that he "come to stop the noise".' Indeed, he goes on, the Conference did in fact issue a warning in 1820 against 'false fire or wild unwarrantable conduct'.

The warning was issued before Billy's conversion. When he joined Hicks Mill chapel over four thousand of the six thousand Bible Christian membership was found in Cornwall and Devon – and the Cornish were a people who did not take easily to restraint. Their Celtic heritage, even without any charismatic leanings in the Christian sense, was charismatic in its own right. Add 'charisma' to 'Celt', leave aside the inbuilt self-restraints of formal education, class gentility and urban society, and the after-meeting was inevitably almost corybantic in character. The truth was that in a community without amenities other than the beerhouse or the coffee-shop, where poverty, sickness, early death and the hardest of hard work were the daily experience of most people, they had very little 'on earth' to shout about. When God, salvation, inward peace and joy and heaven became real to them the effect was explosive. They could not restrain themselves and could see no reason why they should. Early in the morning at the class-meeting, and late at night in the after-meeting they exulted, loudly, freely and often all together, in the experience they shared

But the 'noise' came not only from these causes. Half-a-dozen people might well be praying in one part of the room for one sinful man or woman seeking to be free of his sins while a second group was praying in another part. Add to this the loudly expressed anguish of the sinner in one place and the emphatic shouts of triumph in another where the sinner had 'won through' and it is easy to understand why the neighbours complained! Nevertheless, even the neighbours were without most of the well-trained inhibitions about emotion which our own time knows so well

But it would be easy to get the whole activity of the Church out of proportion. Even by the middle of the century there were only ten thousand Bible Christians in Devon and Cornwall. True there were far more Wesleyan Methodists and a good many staunch Anglicans, as well as the growing strength of the Primitive Methodists. Yet that left a very large proportion of Cornish miners, farmers and fishermen untouched by the Church in any of its forms. The small number of Roman Catholics left practising in the county and the occasional Quaker made little difference to the number. The mass of the people had no genuine religious experience.

It is easy to understand, therefore, the Bible Christian emphasis on 'revivals'.

The denomination grew by the witness and personal evangelism of individuals. Its numbers, at the same time, were increased even more by the 'revivals' which were initiated, in human terms, by the work of the visiting preacher or missioner. Indeed, it has been stated with some authority that in its first half-century the church grew through a succession of revivals, year after year. Nowhere was this more evident than in Cornwall.

William Haslam, the vicar of Baldhu, the parish in which Twelveheads and Kerley Down eventually found themselves, and whose conversion gave Billy so much joy, wrote the story of his life in a book called *From Death to Life*. He was to become a charismatic figure in his own right and it is not surprising that he understood the revivalism of Cornwall. He has an important passage in his book.

'Cornish revivals were things by themselves. Every year, in one part or another, a revival would spring up, during which believers were refreshed and sinners awakened. It is sometimes suggested that there is a great deal of the flesh in these things – more of this than of the Spirit. I am sure this is a mistake, for I am quite satisfied that neither the Cornish nor any other people could produce revivals without the power of the Spirit, for they would never be without them if they could raise them at pleasure. But, as a fact, it is well-known that revivals begin and continue for a time and that then they cease as mysteriously as they had begun.'

A very revealing account of such a revival is included in F. W. Bourne's *The Bible Christians*, and part of its relevance here is that it began in the last of the three chapels which Billy Bray built – Great Deliverance chapel at Carharrack. It was only a couple of years since it had been built when 'there was an extraordinary revival'.

'The work broke out at the Lady-Day Quarterly Meeting, when the power of God took hold of every heart. Many who were not present were affected at the same time.'

The preachers were Henry Reed, Joseph Snell and John Penny, all well-known ministers of the Bible Christian denomination. And there can be no doubt that Billy Bray himself was in the heart of all that happened, every moment he could escape from the mine, running and dancing the three miles or so from Twelveheads to Great Deliverance as fast as he could go, and never silent for a single step of the way.

His 'Glory! Glory!' must have rattled between the chimney-stacks of the mines as he jumped along, over-sounding the noise of the donkey-engines by their sides.

'Every day during that week people in bitter anguish of soul left their work in the hope of finding Christ at the chapel. Many of them were made unspeakably happy in the love of God. On the Sunday morning following it was intended to hold an experience meeting (a testimony meeting) but the anxious enquirers were so numerous, and their cries for mercy so piercing, that the workers were fully engaged all day, and far into the night. The next morning people were at the chapel before daybreak, and the work went on all day without intermission. On Tuesday, the people were there in greater numbers than ever and, it seemed, in deeper distress of soul and it was supposed that by one o'clock twenty persons had stepped into the glorious liberty of the children of God.

'The revival went on for about a month, during which time scores and hundreds were converted. Many Methodist (that is Wesleyan) friends entered into the work as heartily as if they were Bible Christians and reaped, with the hearty goodwill of all concerned, much of the fruit of the revival.'

Two years later the Bible Christian Conference, meeting in Truro where memories of the Great Deliverance revival were still very vivid indeed, asked itself the reasons for the revivals which had been known all over the country. Their answers are interesting. They were: (1) Earnest prayer, sometimes accompanied by fasting, (2) Prayer-meetings after preaching, (3) Protracted Meetings and (4) Inviting people under religious impressions during meetings to come to a certain part of the chapel, men in one pew and women in another, that prayer might be made for them.

How closely Billy Bray fitted into these conditions is clear.

Certainly he exemplified the joys and disciplines, enjoined by other meetings of the Conference, which were part of the life of his Church.

'You praise the Lord, and I'll praise the Lord,' he would sometimes say in company. Or, more pictorially and typically, 'I'll tell 'ee what. You be the parson and call out "Praise the Lord" and I'll be the clerk and answer "Amen". And then you can be the clerk and say "Amen" when I do call "Praise the Lord". And so we can go, all the way home!'

Even more familiar was the end of his conversation with the preacher, Mr Gilbert, who told him of his mother's dancing for joy at Twelveheads. At the end of the evening they spent together at Tywardreath, Billy rose to leave, with a young man who had come with him. 'Johnny, here, and me – we'll make the valleys ring with our singing on the way home.'

'You're a singer, too, then, Billy?' asked the preacher with a smile.

'Aw, yes, bless the Lord, I can sing. Not so sweetly as some, but my Father likes to hear me sing. He do like to hear the crow as well as the nightingale, for he made them both, didn't 'ee?'

Still more often quoted was his remark in a friend's house in Falmouth. 'I can't help praising the Lord. I can't stop, even if I do try to. As I go along the street when I do lift up one foot it do shout "Glory!" and when I do put it down and lift up the other it do shout "Amen". And it do go on like that the whole time I'm walking along!'

He might have added that both feet and body shouted even more loudly when he grew so ecstatic that he danced along instead of walking.

With the joys went the disciplines, as some would regard them, urged by the denomination's leaders. One was fasting – surely a discipline to some, though not perhaps so great in a hungry county as in other places. Another was responsibility to witness personally of Christ to others. What many people found difficult because they did not easily speak of their own experiences – and Billy and other Bible Christians took this as a sign of spiritual 'deadness' – he did naturally, gladly and constantly. By his own witness his wife, his brothers and sisters and his own children were all transformed into exultant or at the least warm-hearted and faithful Christians. He spoke as readily to strangers on the road as he did to his fellow-miners above or below ground, and his words were often as searching, pungent and pithy as they were in the pulpit. What seem to us to be perhaps no more than quaint phrases were born out of the context in which people worked and lived, or expressed in the everyday Cornish speech which held so many of the phrases and so much of the Elizabethan grammar of the Authorised Version of the Bible. It was vividly meaningful to his hearers, when he talked of holding the tempter at bay, to urge them to 'hitch 'en up to the capstan and tighten the rope right up'. The 'capstan', in mining terms, was the wheel and drum which held the rope that drew the buckets of ore up the mine.

Sometimes, however, his scriptural references got mixed with his own imagery. This happened when he broke out with an interjection when the mistress of the house where he was staying was reading the story of the temptation of

Jesus. She reached the point at which the devil offered him the kingdoms of the world if he worship him.

'The auld vagabond!' roared Billy. 'He give away the kingdoms of the world, all of 'em, when he hadn't even an old 'tater skin to call his own, the auld vagabond!'

He was just as pungent in his estimate of people he met, and there is an example of this from an occasion when he was 'missioning' in the Penzance circuit with a friend. They were given bed and board by one of the families belonging to the chapel where they were preaching. Very early, before daylight, Billy was out of bed, leaving his companion in it to watch him leaping, dancing and shouting praises round the tiny room as he so often did in his own cottage.

'Billy, be quiet, do! You'll disturb the family.'

Billy stopped for a moment, and leaped up again. 'So they should be disturbed. They may lie and sleep any time they like and let their wheels go rusty, but while I'm here I shall see they're awaked to get their wheels oiled and be ready for the Lord's work.' He dropped to his knees and began to pray in his ringing voice for every member of the household, ending his petitions with a prayer for his friend who was still in bed. '. . . and have mercy on him, Lord, and make him a better man than he do appear to be!'

It seems a harsh judgment on a fellow-preacher whose fault was that he disliked getting up before dawn and whose virtue was a regard for the convenience of his host.

But Billy can seldom have been an easy bed-fellow.

There was one matter, however, on which the normally vociferous Billy was surprisingly reticent. In view of the generally charismatic nature of the Bible Christians in their earlier history it is perhaps equally surprising that the Conference appears seldom to have mentioned it. This was healing through prayer.

One instance he records he could not have doubted, for it was his own child who was ill and Joey had no doubt she would die. Poor people only turned to the doctor in extremities but this time Joey urged her husband to go and fetch him, or at least – which was more likely to happen, for doctors in mid-century had little time to spare for cottage-visits – to get some medicine from him. He set off, taking the 'eighteenpence which was all the money in the house'.

Billy seldom considered consequences even when they stared him in the face. This time, as he rushed for the doctor, he met a man whose cow had died and he was about the roads begging money to buy another. Touched as always by immediate need he gave the money away – and then wondered what to do next.

"Twas no use going to doctor without money, for he wouldn't give me anything. The only thing was to tell Father about it, so I jumped over the hedge to speak to him. Whilst I was telling the Lord I felt sure the child would live, so I jumped back again and ran away home. As I came in through the door I said, "Joey, the little maid's better, en't she?" "Yes", said Joey, unable to believe it.

"I knew 'twould be so. Father told me so." And only then did he dare tell Joey that he had given away the doctor's money to help buy a cow.

Towards the end of his life, on one of his many special preaching visits – for he was in demand all over Cornwall – he was at Kestle Mill, near the fishing village of Newlyn to hold a 'teetotal meeting' in a Wesleyan chapel. 'A man they called "grandfather" who lived in Newlyn who was very lame, wanted to go with me, but when we'd gone some little way he said he wouldn't be able to go on, he was so lame.

'I said to him "Father must heal you." So then I looked up to heaven and said, "Dear Father, heal him."

'At that "grandfather" said, "All my pain is gone!", and he went on to Kestle Mill as fast as I could go.'

'A week after that "grandfather" rose from his seat in the Wesleyan chapel and told all the people how the dear Lord had healed him the Monday before and he'd never felt any pain since.'

On another occasion Billy spoke of 'Brother Hicks, who'd been in bed for seven years, and for two of them he hadn't been able to speak. And yet, when a brother said that he wouldn't cease praying for him until he could speak, the Lord brought him out in one day!'

His longest and most detailed story concerned Florence Hoskin, of Porthleven, a small fishing village in Mount's Bay. 'She was made a cripple by the way her family had ill-used her and since she had lost the use of one leg she had to use a stick and an old crutch. The doctor told her she would never be well again. But that doctor was wrong.

'The Saturday night before the first Sunday in July, in 1844 I think it was, she went to bed greatly cast down. But she prayed away until the cloud broke from her mind and was made happy in the love of Jesus. Then she said, "Lord, thou hast healed my soul. Why wilt thou not heal my body, too?" When she said so the Lord said to her, "Arise and go down to the chapel-house, and thou shalt be healed." Then she said, "Why not be healed here?" for she was in bed and bed is an easy place for a cripple. But when she said so the Lord's Spirit was taken away from her. So then she said, "I will go to the Gospel-house or anywhere else, only let me be healed." Her Lord said to her, "If I heal thee here they will not believe it, for there are many of them so unbelieving as the Jews in Jerusalem."

'When she got downstairs it was as if the devil tempted her to have her breakfast first, but she said, "No, devil, I will not, for there have been many times when thou hast tempted me to stay for breakfast and I have had a dead meeting through being late." So she went from home a cripple, with her crutch and stick, dragging her lame foot behind her. When her class-leader asked her why she was so early she replied, "Great things are going to be done here today. I am going to have a sound leg, for the Lord has told me so." Her class-leader told her she was mad. But she had faith to believe, and when the meeting was over she could walk away home without a crutch or a stick. And when it was said that Florence Hosken was walking round the Bryanites' chapel without crutch or stick a great multitude of people came together to see what a miracle the dear Lord had wrought – and she never wanted either of them more while she lived.'

In the main, however, the healing in which Billy most, and most often, exulted, was seen in spiritual and moral redemption rather than physical renewal. For him, like physical healing, this was closely linked with faith and prayer, either in the person concerned or through others. No story better fits the case than that of William Haslam, the vicar of Baldhu, whose story is told in his autobiography *From Darkness to Light*. He was in himself a charismatic figure, and Billy Bray breaks abruptly and with typical abandon into the story.

11

The Ecstatic Puritan

Like all miners, Billy moved where there was work. Mines
were closed as the profits slimmed down, shafts were left
deserted and the engine-houses crumbled. But at the same
time, as the demand for tin and copper grew, new shafts
were sunk and new enterprises begun round west Cornwall
and in the centre of the county. What today looks as though
it has always been farming country – and not very good
farming at that – was, a century ago, pock-marked with
pits. Such places as Tywardreath and St Blazey, near St
Austell, and St Neots, in the folds of the undulating moorland near Bodmin, were busy mining-areas in the middle of
the nineteenth century. Billy Bray lived in all of them, working as miner or sometimes 'sub-captain' as employment
offered.

As his family grew up and married some of them moved,
too, to the same parts of mid-Cornwall. All this helped to
make him well-known in a wider area, for while he was
transferred to other circuits and his name was placed on the
'preaching plans' of the places where he lived, he was increasingly in demand as a special preacher on Sundays, or a
'missioner' for longer periods.

Yet it is probably true that his heart was always in the
place where he had been born and grew up. The tiny chapel
which his grandfather had built at Twelveheads, extended

and renewed, his own Bethel and his familiar 'Three-Eyes' at Kerley Downs with Great Deliverance at Carharrack and, above all, the heart of so much Bible Christian life and activity, Hicks Mill chapel – these would always be for him the places where he had found life and proved his faith. It was to Twelveheads that he came back and there that he died. His memorial stands in the churchyard at Baldhu, a tall obelisk above his grave.

But Baldhu church was not built when Billy moved to mid-Cornwall to find new work. Indeed, on those slopes of the downs near Twelveheads there was nothing at all.

Twelveheads was not merely the scene of his childhood and his conversion. His mother lived there until she died and his brother James, whose grave also is at Baldhu, remained there. Billy kept in touch with them and went back 'home' from time to time.

It was while he was living in Twelveheads that he had a word from the Lord. Walking over the rough ground, possibly on his way to Kerley Downs, there came a sudden conviction that God was speaking to him. The words were clear.

'I will give thee all that dwell on this mountain!'

Immediately he dropped to his knees in the rough grass and claimed the fulfilment of the promise. Not that it was much of a mountain, though from the slope of the hill the cottages below, and the smoking mine-stacks round about them, were clear in the hazy morning. Nor were 'those that dwelt on the mountain' anything like the excited scores of people who could sometimes be found at Kerley Downs chapel a mile or so away. Indeed, there were only three cottages to be seen. Nevertheless he set out to fulfil his own part of the bargain. It seemed to him that if *he* did his part then God would 'give him' the cottagers.

He began to visit the cottages, facing them with God's promise, backing this up with his own experience of God's grace, and offering them salvation. This he did again and again, until at last 'the cottages on the mountain' were captured for Christ.

Even then it did not seem very much of a victory for so large-sounding a promise. He fell to his knees in the grass once more. "Tis as you said, Father. You have given me these people. But that bain't much to shout for, is it, Father? There bain't no more than three houses all told!'

He put his head on one side, as if he were listening, as indeed he was.

'There'll be more than these three here? When, Father?' To that he got no answer, but it did not prevent his praying for the fulfilment of the promise when the time came. That it would come he had no doubt. Nevertheless, when he left the Twelveheads district to move to mid-Cornwall still only the three cottages were dotted about the fields. No one had even claimed the traditional Cornish right to a 'plat', an open piece of land, provided he heaved up the walls of a cottage and covered it with a bit of thatch between darkness and dawn. Billy moved on, and went on praying.

It was years later that he had a letter from home, from his brother James. He clutched the letter and began leaping round the room. This was news indeed. They were 'planting' the hill and building a new parish church. Much later came another letter saying that, beside the new church, they were building a school – a sign of the new mid-century spread of education in the mining community – and a house. This was no cottage, but a substantial granite-built home for the new vicar when he came.

Billy went on praying and waited for more news. *This* must be the house, and the people within it, which God had promised him. He waited to be told that the church was to be opened and the vicar installed. Then, at last, brother James wrote to say that services had begun in the church. Now was the moment to go and see what God had done.

He went home to Twelveheads and bounded up the hill on Sunday towards the new parish church. Its freshly-quarried granite was clean and sparkling and the spire cut into the clouded sky. Inside the smallish, tidy, building there was an air of quietness, contrasting with the busy bustle of Billy's more familiar Bible Christian chapels. William Haslam, the new vicar, appeared in his robes and began the service with cool solemnity as Billy shuffled in his seat.

'The Lord haven't given me *his* house!' he muttered to himself. Here was no vision, no freedom, no freshness – this man was a 'Puseyite', a High Churchman of the type then appearing all over England. Billy had not heard of the Oxford Movement in any way that made sense to him, but this restrained, ordered form of worship which derived from it left him depressed and dispirited. He went dejectedly from the new church.

'I don't believe I should have come,' he said to his brother James. 'I don't believe Father told me to come at all. That man haven't got no spirit. But I shall go on tellin' Father that he promised me *all* that dwell on the mountain, and that includes *he*!' He sniffed disparagingly, and went back to St Neots. Before he got home he was leaping once more, sure that the time would come.

The years passed and William Haslam continued to preach the word as he believed it. There was no salvation outside the Church, and that meant the Church of England. Through uncovenanted mercies others might find it – but surely not such Dissenters as Wesleyans or, still further beyond hope, the Bible Christians with their wild ways and restrictive doctrine. Then his gardener fell ill. Haslam describes him as 'not exactly my spiritual child in the gospel but my ecclesiastical child in churchmanship who upheld me in a place abounding with "gospel men" against Dissenters of various kinds.' But, afraid to die, for he had 'galloping consumption', and unhelped by Haslam's ministration, he 'ventured to send for some Dissenter to talk to him and pray with him'. There is a wryness in Haslam's description of the whole event. 'I went to reclaim him, but instead of lying on a bed of suffering the man was walking about the room, praising God in a most joyful state ... It was a great disappointment!'

The gardener, healed by prayer and full of emotion and happiness, tried to witness to his new-found faith. 'I will pray for you while I live, for the Lord to save your soul', he promised his vicar.

A fellow-clergyman of his own Church, whom he consulted, gave Haslam the same message and the same promise, to his discomfiture rather than his consolation.

The following Sunday, filled with unease, he went into the pulpit and announced his text. 'What think ye of Christ?' he asked. What followed was dramatic, for this was a conversion not in the pew but in the pulpit. All at once his soul 'was as full of joy as it had been of misery'. The fervour and earnestness with which he 'proclaimed a present salvation caused many to cry for mercy and many of his parishioners were saved.' The account of what happened was William Haslam's own, written very fully in his autobiography. So, too, is the account of how Billy Bray erupted once more into Baldhu.

A letter reached him at St Neot's from brother James. 'Parson Haslam is converted!' wrote James. 'I think he would like to see you – or so he says.' No more, indeed, than Billy wished to see the parson, and some three months after his conversion the vicar was startled to hear a noise in the hall.

'... someone walking about the hall, praising the Lord. I rose from the breakfast table,' writes Haslam, 'and opened the door to see who my happy, unceremonious visitor could be – and then, for the first time, beheld this queer-looking man. I asked him who he was. He replied, with a face beaming with joy, "I'm Billy Bray – be you the parson?"

' "Yes," I answered.

' "Converted, are 'ee?"

' "Yes, thank God."

' "Be the missus converted?"

' "Yes."

' "Thank the dear Lord", said he, coming into the room and making a bow to the said missus. Then he enquired of her if she had any maids in the house.

' "Yes, there are three."

' "Be they converted?"

' "Yes."

' "Where be they?"

' "In the kitchen."

'So he proceeded to the kitchen, and soon we heard them all praising the Lord in Cornish style in a loud voice.

'After a time Billy joined us again in the dining-room to take, by invitation, some breakfast. But before he sat down he approached me and suddenly put his arm round me, and took me up, and carried me round the table and then, setting me on my chair, he rolled on the floor for joy, and said he was "as happy as he could live".'

Billy told Haslam and his wife why he had come. He had heard of their conversion and had 'been begging Father for leave' to visit them. He 'received permission' just as he was getting into bed at half-past eleven, had got dressed again, hitched the slow old donkey into the cart, left St Neots at midnight, and had made his way through the cold January night to Baldhu 'singing all the way'.

Father had at last fulfilled his promise. They that dwelt on the mountain were his. Prayer was answered and everywhere he looked there was glory.

It is not surprising that a countryman whose home was never anything more luxurious than a cottage and whose prized possession was a donkey-cart rather than a pony-trap should have no time for 'earthly pleasures' and little patience with those who desired to emulate 'the ways of the world'. In this, however, he was not so much expressing a personal viewpoint as echoing the considered judgments of his own Church. The Bible Christians for half a century or more were suspicious of worldliness, particularly as it was expressed in dress or diversions. It was not a new standpoint. The monastics, the preaching orders of St Francis of Assisi and, more recently, John Wesley whom Billy Bray revered, had all reacted in favour of simplicity, self-discipline and 'modesty' and against artificiality and self-indulgence.

At the Conference of 1832 at Lake, in Devonshire, the Bible Christians were all enjoined to practise the puritan virtues and, in particular, the preachers were urged to 'a greater degree of simplicity'. 'Singleness of heart and eye' was to be their chief aim and the Conference singled out one matter for special attention. The wearing of double-breasted coats was unanimously condemned! It smacked of aping the world.

Billy Bray had no money for such novelties, in any case, but he pressed the puritan standpoint on his hearers.

Men came in for rebuke because of 'their airs and graces', and because they chose to spend their money on 'fine dress' – no doubt including the double-breasted coats forbidden to the ministers. He would set his rugged, clean-shaven face in severity as he condemned 'they men who spend more time oiling their "cobs" and twirling their whiskers than they do in saying their prayers and reading their Bibles.' Women, too, were the butt of his caustic country-wit. 'All you women who carry flowers about in your hats! I wouldn't mind you having a wagonload of them on your heads if they would do any good, but they don't do nobody no good at all. And besides' – he would lean confidentially towards some of the offending members of the congregations – 'I thought you would have knowed that flowers only grow in soft places!' The sniggers of the godly must have been worse than the words of the preacher.

As he grew older, and men's fashions changed once more, another thing infuriated him. In his youth and middle age the custom was for men to be clean-shaven or to have no more than a fringe of beard round their chin and jaw-line. He himself had neither. Then came the new craze for full beards. 'I could put up with it if you did do it for the sake of your health,' Billy harangued, 'if it would save you getting a cold or a catch in the chest. But 'tis only for pride and fashion!'

What was worse, the preachers were falling to the common temptation. 'I don't know what the preachers are coming to,' he lamented in their company one day.

'What's wrong with a beard, Mr Bray? It grows by nature, surely?'

Billy snapped round.

'I didn't know you were such a fool as to leave things to grow to their natural state. Do you leave your fruit-trees to grow wild, as nature lets them? I always thought you pruned them!'

Narrow though he was Billy usually managed to get the last word. Repartee was a talent he had never lost since his unregenerate days. Yet, at the same time, this rigidity in small things which to him were matters of conscience was matched by his inflexible integrity in larger issues.

'Fringe benefits' are no modern invention and Billy would probably have regarded most of them as plainly dishonest. His fellow-miners found his unbending attitudes more than irritating, for he questioned activities which were taken for granted by many of them, and which must undoubtedly have been known to sub-captains who had probably indulged in them in their time. One of the most common was due to the way in which wages were paid. On 'setting-days', when a group of miners bid for a particular 'pitch', they agreed what their payment would be, knowing fairly well what the expectation of ore would be where they were working. If it went much above what they expected to extract the 'tributer' who assessed it would get a good proportion of the proceeds. The next month's 'core' however, might be much less profitable because the amount and quality of the tin or copper ore happened to be poorer. To balance things out the miners working in a good pitch would not send it all to the surface but would hide some of it away until the next month's work, or the month after that if necessary, in order to bring up their earnings for that particular month. To Billy this was plain dishonesty, and no arguments would persuade him otherwise.

'And some of those who do it are professors of religion! 'Tis a disgrace!' he would explode. 'You can't be a Christian and a rogue at the same time! What'll happen to 'ee when you do stand before the judgment-seat?'

Though he tried to expostulate and persuade rather than lose his temper, he nevertheless rubbed raw those whom he condemned for these and other practices which seemed to the average man to be no more than common-sense. He may have had a strong following in the chapels where he preached with such verve, but he was not guaranteed the same easy hearing and lack of opposition where he worked.

'We don't want no preaching down here,' was the common verdict. 'Preach where you're planned to, and leave us alone. Go your own way – and leave us to go ours!'

Despite the devoted work and witness of devoted Christians in all the churches it would be a distortion of the facts to suggest that even the recurrent revivals in Bible Christian and Wesleyan chapels resulted in any wholesale turning to faith and change of life in the mass of the population. That not a few *were* truly changed must be seen as a triumph of grace in a society where many people were unchurched, some attended worship out of habit rather than conviction, and the evidences of real conversion were unmistakable.

If, amongst the Bible Christians, charismatic behaviour appeared as one of those evidences there were other characteristics which differentiated them, too. Clearly, from Billy's own criticisms, not all who sat in the pews followed a simple style of life from choice but, in general, the Bible Christians stood firm by the puritan tradition. There were no formal rules forbidding smoking or drinking, for instance, but there was a general acceptance that a man was better without them. Billy himself had no doubt about these matters. He had indulged in both and to break with them was a sign of his liberation when he was converted. But he did not give up either at once.

'I had been a smoker as well as drunkard,' he says, 'and I used to love my tobacco as well as I loved my meat, and I would rather go down the mine without my dinner than without my pipe. But then I heard a voice speaking to me, telling me it was an idol. "Worship the Lord with clean lips," said the Spirit.

'Then the Lord sent a woman, Mary Hawke, to convince me. I was visiting a house and took out my pipe to light it at the fire when Mary said, "Don't you think 'tis wrong to smoke?" So I took the baccy out of my pocket and threw it in the fire, and took the pipe out of my pocket (it would have been a clay one) and ground it under my feet, ashes to ashes and dust to dust.'

Tobacco, however, could still be a comfort. In the last century it was probably chewed as much as it was smoked, and lasted longer! But the same phrase came again. 'I was at a prayer-meeting at Hicks Mill when I heard the Lord say to me, "Worship me with clean lips." So I took the quid out of my mouth and whipped 'en (threw it) under the form. But then, when we got on our knees again, I took out another quid and put that in my mouth. So the Lord said it again. "Worship me with clean lips." So I took the quid out of my mouth once more and whipped 'en under the form and said, "Yes, Lord, so I will!" And I've never smoked nor chewed since.'

At one point he told his congregation (and indeed probably told more than once) how much money he had been able to give away by saving sixpence a week on tobacco. But that there was no general prohibition on smoking is shown by the fact that not a few of the ministers loved their pipes as much as Billy had loved his own. He found this intolerable, for he had the convert's intransigent attitude to 'sins' which he himself had forsworn.

In one Cornish town Billy and another preacher were holding a preaching mission. Billy opened the meeting, not with a hymn as is the modern custom, but with prayer – and not a generalised prayer, either. His fellow-preacher responded with the usual 'Amens' and was joined by the congregation. Billy went on, more pointedly.

'Help the people here to give up their idols!'

'Amen!' responded his colleagues.

'Help them to give up their feathers and ribbons.'

'Amen!'

'Help them to give up their cups and drinking.'

'Amen!'

'Help them to give up their pipes and tobacco.'

Silence from his fellow-preacher.

Without breaking his prayer-style Billy said loudly, '"Amen" to the drinks and cups, but no "Amen" to the pipes and tobacco? You were hearty enough and loud enough with your "Amens" for other people's idols, but you're not willing to part with your own. That it, is it? But, bless the Lord, *I* have!' And he went on with his prayer.

If there was no formal ban on alcohol amongst the Bible Christians, within the first twenty years or so there was a strong movement towards abstaining. In 1837 James Thorne, one of the leaders of the Church, visited London and the Bible Christian stations in Kent, and what he saw convinced him of the need for abstinence. On his return to Devon he founded the first Bible Christian Temperance Society in the village of Langtree. That was on 2nd May. Thomas Tregaskis, who knew Billy Bray well, signed the pledge at Bodmin the same month and, the following year, shared in

Total Abstinence meetings in Truro. On 23rd January, 1838, Tregaskis and James Teare held a meeting at Hicks Mill. 'Thirty-eight signed the pledge, and kept it to their lives' end.'

The first to do so was Billy Bray.

From that time onwards he gave himself unremittingly to the cause of total abstinence. He knew well from experience, his own and those whom he had grown up with and worked with, the devastation that drinking wrought in families aready poorly paid, and he probably spoke as frequently at Temperance meetings as he did at revival meetings. It needs to be said that this was not a popular cause in Cornwall or elsewhere in church circles. Wesleyan Methodists were divided at this period whether to accept a candidate for the ministry who declared himself a total abstainer, and the criticism of Wesleyans in St. Ives who declared for total abstinence was so strong that they actually seceded and called themselves the 'Teetotal Methodists'. St Ives, indeed, still has a narrow street in the fishing port called 'Teetotal Street'. The Bible Christians were notable, and often unpopular, because they were willing to allow their chapels to be used for meetings advocating this unpopular cause.

Billy Bray, speaking all over the county in his own vivid style, never left anyone in doubt that he thought 'the old devil gets at people through drink even if he can't get them any other way – and by drink he'll get them down to hell where they'll starve with thirst for ever.'

In 1838 the Bible Christian Conference adopted a resolution recommending 'our brethren in the ministry and such other friends as may feel disposed to unite with us, to devote the forenoon of each Friday to abstinence and special prayer to God for the prosperity of his work among us, and especially to observe the quarterly fasts on the first Friday after each quarter day.'

Billy Bray had anticipated, and exceeded, this recommendation, and continued to do so to the end of his life.

Sometime after his conversion he pondered what he might do more than he was already doing. He received this answer. Fast this day for the Lord's sake.'

'I will, Lord,' he answered, and took no food until eight o'clock that night. 'This was the best day I had had for twenty-nine years,' he commented, later.

He was not a man to keep anything to himself, and he soon told his neighbours what had happened. Going without food because there was none in the house was one thing, and a common deprivation for some families. But going without for some obscure spiritual reason was quite another, and his friends were sure he would do himself harm. One friend took him to task.

''Tis the devil trying to starve thee out, for he knows what great things God has done for thee.'

'No such thing, Richard,' answered Billy. 'The devil shall not starve me for I shall ask the Lord if I'm doing right, or no.'

The next Sunday morning, kneeling on a stool, he prayed aloud. 'Lord, thou knowest what people are saying, that I shall starve myself if I fast. Now, my dear Lord, if I must not fast make me happier than I have been while I fasted.'

Nothing happened, and he put the question directly. 'Lord, must I fast?'

'Then,' he records, 'the power of God came upon me, so that I fell off the stool, and I was convinced that it was the will of the Lord that I should fast.'

His decision affected his observance of Sunday profoundly for the rest of his life. There was hardly a Sunday, except towards the end, when he did not preach, and often he was many miles from his own home. This involved his rising early and walking anything up to twenty miles or more to reach his appointment. 'Walking' is an inadequate word. Those who saw him or met him found him tripping and jumping, running and dancing as he made his way. When he reached his preaching-place he threw himself completely into worship, praying and preaching at length and always with tremendous vitality.

Yet he never broke his fast before he left home, nor did he eat a midday meal. Instead of eating and resting he set off to visit the sick as soon as the service was over, coming back to preach again at a second service.

His friends and hosts would urge him to eat, but he refused in more or less the same terms every time. 'On a Sunday I get my breakfast and my dinner from the King's table, and I would not exchange this food from heaven for the richest dinner on earth.'

The puritan spirit and the ecstasy of the spirit were mixed together in him. For Billy, truly, 'his meat was to do his Father's will'.

12

Heaven is my Home

'Here he comes,' muttered the youth. 'Hush,' he went on as his companions began to giggle. 'We shan't scare 'en if you do make that noise.'

Billy's preoccupation with the devil was known to everyone who heard him and the group of boys, shuffling above the road, planned to make capital out of it. In the dark night they were gathered on top of a typical Cornish hedge, high and topped with trees, with the narrow road well below them. They heard Billy's feet tapping as he jogged along the lane, murmuring to himself. Suddenly they broke out into groans and screeches as he reached them. Billy stopped and looked up. The horrible noise was redoubled. Would he run away?

'Billy Bray! 'Tis the devil come for 'ee!'

A cheerful voice came up from the foreshortened figure below. 'Aw, you, is it? You're some long way off tonight, aren't 'ee, devil? I thought you was usually down here alongside me!' The deflated boys crawled down as the little man went on his way down the lane, and they heard him singing as he disappeared between the high hedges. It was not the first time someone had tried that particular trick on him, and he would have said he knew the devil's voice well enough not to mistake it.

But, for Billy, though his tempter might come and go,

might indeed be a 'long way off' at times, there was always a splendid immediacy about the presence of God. Doubts came and went, problems and sorrows were a natural part of life, there was some ebb and flow in the depth of his experience, but he seems never to have been stranded high and dry, out of reach of the tide of the spirit. It was partly due, no doubt, to the simplicity of his faith and the unsophistication of his nature and background but he had an unshakable conviction of God's presence with him. 'Father' would never lose hold of him. Equally, he was assured of joy to come – 'Heaven' was 'home', and it was the word he increasingly used for it as he grew older.

These inalienable certainties were the background to one of his most persistent activities. He was at least as busy in 'visiting' as he was in evangelism. He found happiness in visiting the godly, many of them simple people like himself, because they could talk the same language, much of it biblical and often highly pictorial. With them, he gained as much as he gave. He called a simple villager, Peggy Mitchell, 'the best scholar in Gwennap parish, because she could read her title to a mansion in the skies', which illustrates his fondness for imagery and his ready, if mixed, memories of Bible and hymn-book.

His visiting had several intentions. He visited the 'saints' for his own benefit as well as theirs, the sinners to call them to repentance, the dying to sustain their hold on heaven and the poor to see if he could give them practical help. If he was a tireless visitor his persistence, with those he wanted to gain, or reclaim if they had ceased chapel-going, must sometimes have been an irritation.

There is a traditional story of his knocking on a cottage door where a housewife had no wish to see him. The small girl who opened the door looked at him innocently. 'Mother's out,' she announced.

Billy looked into the small room and saw a curtain billowing. Clearly the woman had slipped into the 'spence' (the cupboard under the stairs) to avoid him, but her shoes still protruded under the curtain.

He cocked his head quizzically on one side. 'Aw, out is she? Well, next time she do go out, my 'andsome, tell her to take her feet with her!'

It was hard to best him in a situation of that sort.

His visiting, as has been shown already, could often expose bare shelves and empty cupboards, and however little he and Joey might have in their own meagre stores other people's need would seldom go unmet if he had money in his pocket.

He appears to have been remembered most vividly, however, for his 'sick-visiting', and it would seem that such times were hard to forget, in any case, for his approach to a sick-bed was very much his own. One Bible Christian minister recalled an occasion of this kind. The preacher was not only ill, but apparently very near death. His Victorian phraseology is suited to a death-bed scene. 'To all human appearance, I was about to depart from this mortal life. Then the hallowed stillness of my bedroom was broken by the distant sound of the well-known "Hallelujah!" and the jubilant tones of the faithful soul as he mounted the stairs singing:

> "There, there at his feet we shall meet,
> And be parted in body no more!"'

To the boisterous little miner a sick-room was no place for mawkish sentiment or silent commiseration, especially if the person in bed was a Christian.

His biographer, Bourne, insists that he always came with 'tact and discretion' but the description is an overstatement if some of his other stories are accurate. The words cannot, at any rate, have their modern meaning. A better one would surely have been 'realism'. It seems appropriate to one of his visits to a woman in severe pain. 'You're as well off as the Queen, me dear. For the Queen, yesterday is over and done with, and *she* don't have to live it over again. Neether do you. The pain you had yesterday is over and done with, so you won't have *that* pain again! Praise the Lord for *that*!' It was severely realistic comfort. Or, again, only to someone with a firm grasp of heaven would another sick-visit have offered consolation. This was to a poor woman, lying in bed in a single-room cottage, drab and comfortless already, where the thatch-roof had been blown off in a gale.

'The storm never touched *you*, did it, me dear? You can be thankful for *that*! And heaven will seem a handsome place when you do get there. Think what you'll be able to say then. "What a wonderful place this is!" And you'll be able to look down on your cottage with its roof blown away, and little meat on the shelves, and everything all dirty everywhere. And you'll be able to say, "Well *this* is a change for the better, *this* is!"'

With such simple people as these where Billy was offering pastoral care to those whose circumstances of life were undoubtedly much akin to his own, he had an immediate kinship. His words seemed realistic because they would have spoken truly to himself in similar circumstances. His sick-visits were not confined to his own circle, however, and for other occasions his approach was startlingly different.

Not all chapel-goers were poor and some were, by the rural standards of their time, undoubtedly affluent. Billy had the typical attitude of most of his circle to wealth. They suspected that it came from toughness in business or commerce, or shrewd bargains in the market, and the only true test of those who had money was how they used it. Money played its own part in Billy's sermons and addresses. He could make effective and witty play with descriptions of what moths could do to stored-up finery in winter wardrobes, and how rust could corrupt base metal bought for sterling quality silver. 'Money-grubbing' and 'storing up treasures on earth' were easy targets for an impecunious miner with a sharp tongue and an abrasive wit. If the majority of the congregation enjoyed his sallies the more well-heeled did not and, in one chapel, a wealthy house-owner resented them greatly and seldom failed to say so.

It was all the more astonishing, therefore, that when this man lay sick and apparently dying he should have asked his family to get Billy to visit him.

He responded very readily.

This time he did not enter the house shouting 'Hallelujah' as he did when he visited Mr Christophers, the apparently dying minister. Nor did he bound up the well-carpeted stairs above the tidy hall when he was admitted to the house. He walked slowly and trod gently into the bedroom, with its large and opulent furniture and hangings and all its other evidences of wealth and respectability. Inside the room he stopped and looked round slowly, his hat in his hand. He seemed to be awed into silence by what he saw. Then he spoke.

'My dear soul, did Jesus Christ ever occupy such a house as this? Live in such luxury? Lie in so big a bed?'

He paused while the family round the room shuffled awkwardly.

'Did he ever have so much money to spend on carpets and chiffoniers and sheets?'

The family rustled their silks more angrily, and the old man in the bed stiffened and his face grew taut. But Billy went on.

'My dear Lord, *you* never had nothing to call your own, did 'ee? You never had no house, not even a little small cottage. You only had the clothes you stood up in, Lord. Edn't that so? Your mother wasn't dressed in silks and satins, was she, Lord? You couldn't afford nothin' like that, could 'ee?'

Anger turned to embarrassment as Billy went on apostrophising his unseen Master. By the time he had finished, quick to sense change in the emotional atmosphere of the sick-room, the old man's tight face had loosened and he was weeping. Billy went to the bed, dropped on his knees and began to pray in a very different fashion, and then left the room and went down the stairs. By the time he reached the hall one of the daughters was by his side.

'Father says will you come again, Mr Bray? Tomorrow, if you please.'

For more than a fortnight the drab-clothed miner went, staying longer and longer by the old man's bedside, until at last he died in peace.

To this man, with his sharp tongue, his glowing faith and his strange ways and mannerisms, a death-chamber was either a field of triumph already assured, or a battle-ground for souls. If he visited the sick wherever he found them he seems to have been strangely at home in the presence of death. To understand this, with our own awed or embarrassed attitude to death, we need to realise that, for the Victorians, it was a very different matter.

For one thing, death was more common – not that it happened more often, but it happened almost always as part of the immediate experience of any family. Children died younger, often very young indeed, from the same causes that we now associate with less-developed societies – epidemics, fevers, respiratory diseases and malnutrition. They, and older people, died where they lived, in their own homes; or of disasters like mine accidents, or field accidents, but seldom away from home in hospital. At the same time, perhaps paradoxically, it was a significant event rather than a commonplace occurrence, and this was emphasised by the funeral. In towns and amongst those who could afford it, the funeral with its black and shrouded hearse, its black-caparisoned horses and sombrely clad mourners excited both fascinated interest and outward shows of respect for the bereaved. In country areas, and certainly in Cornwall, the funeral was an occasion for the whole community where the coffin was carried shoulder-high and most of the male population 'walked', making a solemn procession from home to church and churchyard. In addition to all this, death was, even for many who seldom made any great profession of faith, a time when the sense of eternity, of a highly-coloured and pictorial image of heaven and hell, could scarcely be escaped.

It is not surprising that for men like Billy Bray, with their Celtic temperament and their highly emotional religious environment, death was of tremendous significance. Billy had lived for years in terror of torment in a physical hell, and had passed from this anguished state to long years of rapturous anticipation of heaven. That he saw it and preached about it in material terms is to say only that he was a man of his time, living in a particular climate of theology and biblical exegesis.

He would tell the sick, and especially the dying, that he hoped to see them in heaven – 'for I hope I *shall* be there one day to see 'ee – dressed in bright and shining robes.' He might add, with a wry humour, that they 'would find it even more trying on the feet to get used to golden shoes than to the last pair they bought in Redruth market'. For the good and godly, death should have no terrors. For those who were left behind the separation should hold no regrets.

'If the Queen were to send for your husband you might be sorry to part with him, but you would go round telling everybody that she'd done so, wouldn't 'ee? And if she was to send for your son, you'd tell it about the whole neighbourhood, sayin' 'twould be the making of 'en. So why shouldn't you be even more happy when the Lord Jesus have sent for 'en? He've been *promoted*!'

For Billy himself death was something he never feared. Going to bed one night in his host's home on one of his preaching visits he prayed with the family and then turned to his host's daughter. 'If you do find me dead in bed in the morning you know what you must do? Stand up and shout "Hallelujah!"'

'I doubt if I should do any such thing, Mr Bray.'

He looked surprised. 'Bless 'ee, my dear, why ever not?

'Twould be only fitty (proper) to do it so loud as you could. *I* should be all right. I should be with Father!'

He was to do it himself, and more, at the moment of his own greatest loss.

His wife Joey, who had married him with little hope of anything more than a plodding and penny-pinching domesticity, punctuated by child-bearing, had found married life even worse than she had ever thought possible. Then, when drunkenness and licence had given place to sobriety and a life of Christian happiness she became Billy's staunchest helper, putting up with his over-generous charity to other people while his own family were in danger of going short of necessities, accepting his new way of life which took him out preaching and away from home on revivals and temperance campaigns. She shared his faith, spoke his language, and brought up his children in the same ways. She moved from her familiar home at Twelveheads as he changed jobs and, though she was never any kind of public figure – there was no competitive charisma in the Bray family – she loved him and supported him in all he did. But, in a society where men usually had a much shorter life than women, Joey would not outlast her wiry and tough husband. She fell ill, and was ill for a very long time, suffering great pain and growing steadily weaker.

At one point in her illness, when she was distressed and unresponsive to Billy's fervent exhortation, he knelt and held her hand.

'Low, are 'ee?' Low in faith as well as strength, he meant.

'Ess, Billy. I should have expected to *see* something of heaven opening up.' She looked at him anxiously. 'People do, don't they, when it gets nearly time to go?'

Billy brushed her unease aside. 'I don't see nothing, neether, me dear. But what need have *we* of sights and signs. If I did *see* the Lord raise Lazarus out of his grave I shouldn't believe it any more than I do now. If I did see 'en raise Jairus's daughter or the widow's son to life I shouldn't have no more faith in it than I have now. If I seen 'en rise up out of the tomb himself I shouldn't believe it any more strongly than I do at this moment. We don't need to *see*, my 'andsome, we do *know*.'

Joey gripped his hand more firmly, and her husband went on. 'We don't need no sight of heaven before we get there. 'Tis there, sure 'nough. Do 'ee believe that, then?'

'Ess, Billy, I *do* believe it!'

Suddenly for him, and for her too, the room was filled with glory rather than with peace, and his 'Hallelujah' rang through the house, echoed by Joey's own quiet praise.

Where Billy was when she died we do not know, but he was not at home. He came soon afterwards and, to the discomfiture of the quieter mourners, bounded up the staircase shouting praises. This was no time for grief. They heard his feet beating on the floorboards as he leapt in ecstatic thanksgiving. 'Glory! Glory!' echoed through the cottage.

'My dear Joey is gone up with the bright ones!' he announced to all he met and his eyes were bright with gladness instead of tears.

If his own passing, when it came, was to be quieter it would be enriched with the same sense of triumphant joy. To Billy, if the devil was real, God was nearer still. Heaven, to him, was home and all earthly life a preparation for it.

13

The Glory Man

In one Cornish family, at least, where the stories of Billy Bray were passed from generation to generation, he had his own apt descriptive title. He was known as 'Billy Bray, the Glory Man'. It is as good a name as any, for it catches something of his ebullient happiness, his ejaculatory style and his awareness of heaven on earth as well as heaven to come. But that first sentence also illustrates the fact that Billy, after his death, became a legend in his own land. The father who told his children, and even more the grandmother who told them, 'I heard Billy Bray' was not only passing on the legend but perhaps assisting it to grow, and ensuring that the little miner became larger in retrospect than he was in life.

A writer, fully sympathetic to the Bible Christian tradition, refers to him as 'that over-rated local preacher, Billy Bray', and suggests that other lay preachers could easily be found in his own period who, while sharing much of his spirit, were more typical of their own Church. Is the adjective just? At this distance it is hard to determine whether he has been over-rated or not. Because he was so intensely individualistic it is difficult to compare him with others, especially when few lengthy accounts of them exist. In some senses, not least the extravagance of his expression, he seems to stand alone.

Was he, then, truly ecstatic or merely eccentric? Was he shrewd in his judgments, or only stubborn and sometimes rude? Did he draw so many hearers because he was convincing or because he was something of a comedian at best and a comic figure at worst? Did his 'shouting' and 'leaping' attract or repel? Was he 'popular' because of his lack of restraint, or in spite of it?

There is a story of another lay preacher, later in the century than Billy Bray, who was 'attacked' after his conversion by two of his past cronies from the mine. One stood on one side of him, the second on the other, arguing and jeering.

'Be 'ee a rogue, Dick Hampden, or only a fool?' asked one.

Dick looked at them for a moment. 'I be midway between the one and the other, I reckon,' he retorted to their defeat and amusement.

'Midway between the two' may well be the answer to many of the questions about Billy Bray, too. He attracted and repelled. He was certainly taken to task, right to the end of his life, by more conservative Christians for his 'disturbances'. At the same time, others tolerated his eccentricities because they never doubted his sincerity. But many who came prepared to criticise were more deeply moved by his conviction than they were amused by his undoubted wit. To say that 'some who came to scoff remained to pray' is not only an understatement; it simply does not represent the case. In his own declaration of the gospel, and by his personal witness, he brought conviction and life to an immensely large number of people. How often he preached without conversion it is, of course, impossible to say, and others gathered a harvest from the seeds he himself sowed on his preaching and missioning visits. But that he expected conversions, and very often saw them, is indisputable.

What is more, he can still leave Christians in our own time wishing that they had something of his ineffable sense of glory in his faith and experience.

His spiritual gifts were added to an innate exuberance of temperament and a natural gift with words. He was as unreserved in his approach to people, even to strangers, as it was possible to be. He loved company, and especially the company of Christian people, but beyond this lack of any sort of shyness was the impulsion of the evangelist. He knew he had something infinitely worth while to share and he wanted to share it with everybody. If he overstepped the boundaries of sobriety in the pulpit or the natural decorum of a saddened household this was only because he remained himself. And it never occurred to him to try to be anything else. He had limitations of knowledge, sophistication, experience of the wider world beyond Cornwall, and culture. If he realised this he did little to mend the situation. His education was minimal – his scrawled and ill-spelt 'journal' reflects both a lack of literacy and an anxiety to get things down and done with as quickly as he could. But he never aped anyone else. He was an 'original' who was content to have a gospel to preach, an experience to share, and no obvious wish to do it in any other way than his own.

It has been suggested that he was little-known until F. W. Bourne wrote *The King's Son*. This may have been true outside Cornwall and South Devon, but there he was probably better-known than any other of his contemporaries. A 'legend' is not created over-night, and Dr Mark Guy Pearse, one of the outstanding Wesleyan Methodist ministers of the late nineteenth and early twentieth century, who was born a year or so before Billy Bray died, reflects the contemporary remembrance of his influence. He may not have seen it himself, but his family must have done and he asserts that 'on Sundays, when one met crowds of strangers making for the little white-washed chapel that was perched up amongst the granite boulders, or when one found the quiet "church-town" thronged by well-dressed people, the usual explanation was that Billy Bray was going to preach.' It was not someone else's memory but his own experience, however, that 'from one end of Cornwall to the other no name is more familiar than that of Billy Bray.'

Methodism, despite its divisions in the last century, was not so rigidly separated that Billy Bray, and others like him, were unwelcome in the pulpits of Wesleyan and Primitive Methodist chapels. He preached on the 'plan' of the circuits in which he lived from time to time, for this he was expected to do. There were few ministers, and lay preachers were essential to the supply of the pulpit in the country chapels. But for many years Billy was in great demand in other places for all kinds of 'specials' – chapel anniversaries, chapel openings, missions, 'revivals' and teetotal meetings were all likely to be well-attended or crowded-out if it were announced that he would preach or speak. Nor was this some sort of local fame.

In 1841 he was not yet fifty and had been a preacher for less than twenty years. It was in October that year that a new Bible Christian chapel was opened in the heart of the 'Bryanite' country at Lake, Shebbear, in Devon. There were three sermons on the opening Sunday, by two distinguished Bible Christian ministers and the Independent minister from Torrington. On the second Sunday, when the great celebrations continued, there were four services, one conducted by the President of the Conference, one by the past President and another by a minister who would soon come to that office. The first service, however, was at six a.m. – and at this service Billy Bray was the preacher. To bring Billy out of Cornwall to Devon and set him with five ministers of distinction implies more than 'reputation'; it indicates that he was felt to have a distinctive message and contribution for such an occasion.

Not that Billy suffered from any delusions of ecclesiastical grandeur. He could not preach like a President of the Con-

ference! And he knew it. On occasions when he was one
speaker amongst a group of men much more distinguished
than himself he would come back to the same analogy.
'You know what John do say in the Book of Revelation
about the New Jerusalem, don't 'ee? Founded on precious
stones it is. Emeralds and amythests, and sapphires and
topaz, and pearls and jasper ... ever seen any of they stones,
have 'ee, my friends? More wonderful than the Queen's
jewels, they are. And now do 'ee know what the King of
Kings have done? He've bent down and picked up a rough
lump of Cornish "spar" (rock) and added it to the foundations alongside all they other precious stones. And that's
why poor old Billy is standin' up here alongside of these
gentlemen who are so much wiser than he is.' He did not
overrate himself, but he believed there was good reason for
his being where he was.

What sort of message did he bring? A very simple one, in
terms that his hearers would understand. He had gone, for
instance, as one of the two special preachers at the reopening
of a chapel after it had been repaired. He preached in the
morning. The other preached in the afternoon and evening
– 'he was filled with the power of God.' They stayed on for
the Monday meetings, a 'tea-meeting' at three o'clock
followed by tea at five, no doubt with pasties and saffron
cake. His comment was caustic. 'I believe we would do better
to fast and pray, and give the money without a tea.' His own
habit was to spend the time visiting when he went away to
preach and not to break his fast until after the last service.
But he complimented the congregation on their repaired and
renovated chapel when he spoke in the evening. 'The Lord
have given 'ee a handsome chapel, and now he do want some
handsome furniture in it.' Before they could exchange
glances after looking at the stained wood benches he went
on. 'Bad furniture is a disgrace in a good house. And you
know what the proper furniture for the Lord's house is?
Not seats and benches, but sanctified souls. Never mind the

old benches. *We* must be made new, and then the Lord will have something to rejoice over when he looks down to see how his house is furnished!'

He has a story – not without its amusing side – of an occasion when he 'dried up' in the pulpit. Every preacher knows the terrible feeling of a sudden and shattering blackout when he cannot remember what he has been saying or what he intended to say next. Billy had his own explanation of why it happened. 'I was at a place on the St Neot's plan, at Redgate, and there was a chapel full of people, and the Lord gave me great power and liberty in speaking. But all at once the Lord took away his Spirit from me, so that I couldn't speak a word.' For Billy, whatever happened was God's doing.

He not only went on again, making the best of a bad job as it were. He made capital out of it. When he had recovered himself he began. 'I'm glad I stopped. My stopping may be the best sermon you ever heard. And I'll tell 'ee for why. First, it has made me more humble. I can't speak unless the Lord gives me the words to speak.

'And then, 'tis good for *you*. You do say that we can all speak when we have a mind to, without the Lord as well as with him. Well, you saw what happened when he took his Spirit from me. I couldn't say another word. And neither can you. You may go on speaking your own words if you have a mind to, but you can't speak the Lord's word without the Lord's Spirit.

'And there's another reason why I'm glad I had to stop. Some of you young men there in front of me may be called to stand up in the pulpit, and if you do stop in the middle like I did you may think 'tis no use going on trying to preach, for you'll only stop in the middle. But now you'll be able to say, "I heard Billy Bray once and *he* stopped because the Lord took his Spirit from him . . . but *he* went on again and so can I!"'

'And then, after that,' records Billy, 'I went on again, and went on a great while, telling the people what the Lord gave me to say.'

There must have been very few Sundays when he was not preaching somewhere until the time when age began to overtake his natural strength – and, for him, bodily energy and a pulpit ministry went together. He was a strict sabbatarian, and refused to ride to his appointments. Even in old age he chose to walk, even if it meant rising very early in the morning to do so and then walking ten or fifteen miles before the service. The donkey-cart could well be put to use if he were going on a weekday, or on a Saturday for a weekend appointment or to begin a week's mission on the Sunday. Otherwise it was his own dancing feet that carried him over the rough roads and rocky tracks through the moorlands or the granite outcrops of the west.

To those who sympathised with him – 'Fancy an old man like you walking all that way, Mr Bray!' – he had a swift reply. 'Old? My dear, I feel as young as a boy!' He would prove it by his irrepressible activity in the pulpit, speaking with his whole body, and his prolonged visitation when the morning or afternoon service was over.

Towards the end of his life he was living again in his home village of Twelveheads, near St Day, but that did not prevent him travelling almost as widely as ever in his evangelistic ministry. He could look back over more than seventy years, and nearly half a century of joyful Christian living. The far-off days when he worked in these same mines, making a mockery of religion while he paused to raise a laugh from his fellow-miners on the same 'core', or making the 'levels' ring with praise and prayer to the astonishment of these same men – all that seemed very far distant and yet, in some moments, extraordinarily near. He had never lost the rapture of those first days of release after months of inner struggle.

It was years earlier that he had put a simple statement of his philosophy to one of the Bible Christian ministers. 'If

Billy gets work, he praises the Lord. When he gets none, he goes on singing all the same. Do 'ee think Father will let Billy starve? No, 'course he won't. No – there'll always be a little, small bit of flour in the bottom of the barrel for 'en. I can still trust Father, and while I trust him he'd as soon starve the archangel Michael as he'd starve Billy!'

It was a certitude that was to continue with the years, although the 'little, small bit of flour in the bottom of the barrel' was all he often possessed.

As he grew into an old man – and for anyone, especially a miner who faced the hazards of rock falls, constant damp and miner's phthisis, to live beyond seventy was to be old indeed – he continued to rejoice as loudly as ever, and as publicly. He was, in these last years without his treasured Joey, greatly supported by his friends. When there were days of weakness in which he could not visit them, they visited him. But the atmosphere and the conversation remained much the same wherever they were.

How little he changed even towards the end of his life is illustrated by a visit to Plymouth. The year was 1867, and Billy was then seventy-three, a time of life arguably intended for reasonable quietness and restraint. On this occasion he was again crossing Methodist boundaries, for his engagements were in Primitive Methodist chapels. It was one of the founders of that Church who had been disturbed by the noisy behaviour of some of Billy's Bible Christian friends many years before in Twelveheads. Time had done much to establish the Primitive Methodists throughout Britain as a radical, politically-aware, evangelical Church. But Billy himself had not changed in the interval. He was the same as ever. With him in the pulpit, pleading for conversion and rejoicing with those who had certainty in their faith, the meetings were noisy, excited and, in Billy's phrase, 'blessed'.

'You really must not make so much disturbance, Mr Bray,' said one critic at the end of a particularly noisy service. 'We don't like it.'

'You mean the old Smutty-Face, the devil, don't like it, I reckon,' snapped Billy. 'If we're not ashamed to do our master's work in the street, we shouldn't be ashamed to praise him in the chapel. If I listened to such as you I should have lost my best friend long ago. That's the dear Lord who have made me glad so that no one can make me sad. He makes me shout, and there is no one that can make me doubt! He makes me dance and leap, and there is nobody that can keep down my feet!

'Why, mister,' he shouted, 'I sometimes feel so full of the power of God that if you was to cut off my feet I believe I should lift up the stumps and go on praising with them!'

There were those who wondered how he could now manage even to lift up his feet! He was growing visibly much older, losing weight from his spare frame, walking more slowly – but talking and praising and exhorting still. At the end of that same year when he missioned in Plymouth amongst the Primitive Methodists he went to Crantock, not far from Newquay, to share in a 'revival' – this time amongst the Wesleyan Methodists – only a week or so after he had got back to Twelveheads from a similar joyful time in Newlyn, near Penzance. Weak as he was, as he poured out exhortation in the pulpit and ejaculations in the meetings afterwards the experience seemed to stimulate him to new vigour. 'The dear Lord made the people very happy, and he made me happy with them', was his own way of putting it.

One night, after the meeting in the chapel ended and the candles were snuffed out, there were those who still wanted to go on in the same exalted mood. It was too cold to stand outside and they went on to the home of one of the local people. Not all had 'triumphed' and there was still work to do. It was a noisy, unfettered occasion. 'Some were singing, some praising, some praying and others crying for mercy, until six more souls gained their liberty.' That it went on until late in the night was something which nobody minded. 'We could do nothing but praise,' said Billy in his reference to what happened, 'for the Spirit was poured out wonderfully. I was as happy as I could be, and live. It was one stream of glory!'

Crantock was a memorable 'last appearance'. He was not to preach again and, indeed, as he grew steadily weaker, he left Twelveheads only once more, to visit his children who were living near his old St Neots home, at Liskeard.

Years before, while William Haslam was still vicar of Baldhu, they had sat talking about their Christian experience. 'How is it you always seem to be on the mountaintop, Billy?' asked the vicar, 'while I find that *my* own experience ebbs and flows?'

'Well, as to that,' responded Billy, ''twouldn't be true to say that I'm always on the heights, neether. I do go down into the depths sometimes, and the old devil do think he've got me at last. But I do come up again. And one reason is, I aren't hindered by too much learnin'.'

'What does that mean?'

'Well, it do say in the Book that we've got to be fools for Christ's sake. Some of 'ee are disadvantaged by havin' so much book-learnin', see? But when you do talk about poor old Billy ... why, I was a fool to begin with!'

Wit and naivety combined to emphasise the truth that became increasingly evident as he moved towards the end – the simplicity of his faith.

If he could no longer busy himself with public work he was not so limited that he could do nothing where he lived. Now, however, he lived for and with his friends; the neighbours who had known him through the years, who had known his old, blind mother, seen his children grow up and listened to his dear wife Joey's complaints – never made with malice – about Billy's generosity to everybody except his own family. These were the people who not only knew what he was talking about, but spoke his own tongue, and could quote the Bible back at him with the same fervent faith as his own.

'I thought, after I'd had breakfast, I would go to see some friends. But after I'd called on some of them I had to go home again. I had hard work to get home, too. I was so ill, and my breath was very short.'

By the beginning of the spring even that exertion was beyond him. He must sit quietly in his cottage and wait for others to come to him.

In the earlier days a Bible Christian minister had talked with him about prayer. Or, rather, had asked him about it, for even the ministers recognised the quality of the 'strange little man', as Haslam had called him. 'How long do I need to pray at a time if I am to keep my soul healthy?' he had asked.

Sitting in his cottage Billy had pointed across at the chimney-piece. 'Do 'ee see that there bit of brass up there that Joey have been polishin'?'

'Yes.'

'Well, mister, if you do give 'en a rub every now and again you'll keep 'en bright and shinin', just like that. Five minutes rubbin' is all it needs. But let 'en go for a while without rubbin' and you'll have a main job to get 'en bright again.'

That had been one of Billy's secrets all his life. He might spend long periods on his knees at times, but he was too impatient a man for over-long devotions when the Lord's work was waiting to be done. There would be a miner's wife in trouble, a man to be seen who had not lately been to chapel, a boy who had recently been converted. But, in all the hustle of living, all the quick jogging and leaping to his preaching appointments, all the 'traipsing' from one house to another, there would still be time for the 'quick rub' on the already polished brass, the swift prayer and the sudden burst of praise.

152

Indeed, as he drew towards the end of his life, 'praising' was the key-note of his prayers and his conversation. And his praises, right to the last, were loud. He might have little energy to go out, but he could still shout. And shout he did, as the record shows. Again and again came the same word.

'Glory!'

His own west Cornish pronunciation gave it an added roundness, made it last longer as he shouted 'Glow-ry! Glow-ry!'

Yet with the ecstasy there was melded a deeper and quieter emotion. It was the almost incredulous happiness of taking the last turn in the road after a long and body-draining trek and seeing your own home only a few hundred yards away ... the awed relief of the man who clambered up the ladder from the mine-shaft escaping from the pit in which the roof had crashed down in the level where he had been working ... the sudden exhilaration which Billy had seen in the worn fishermen of St Ives who had battled back from the Atlantic storms and climbed up from the battered boats to find their families waiting on the quayside. It was the contentment of day's work done, of the load laid down, of coming home.

As the late spring skies grew more brightly blue, as the larks sang and the furze bushes gleamed brilliantly yellow amongst the granite boulders, Billy moved out of spring into the last autumn days of his life.

'I shall soon be going homelong,' he said in his weakened voice. 'Homelong to Father.'

The doctor came to see him towards the end of May. 'How is he?' asked someone standing by the bed.

'He won't last much longer,' said the doctor, and was taken aback by the verve with which the old man shouted aloud.

'Glory!' Then he turned more quietly to the doctor. 'Goin' homelong, am I doctor? I shall soon be with Father, shan't I?' The room was very quiet, and Billy went on.

'Shall I tell Father *you'll* be coming home to 'en one day, doctor dear?'

It was his last simple word of evangelism, and the doctor left the room with glistening eyes.

A day or so later, on 25th May, 1868, William Trewartha Bray went home. He was almost seventy-four. They brought the coffin from his cottage into the 'court' at the front on the Friday and, before his friends carried it from Twelveheads to Baldhu church where he was buried, a Bible Christian minister and a layman, one of Billy's oldest friends, spoke their funeral orations. Everyone who listened could have added his or her own personal reminiscence or testimony.

In the schoolroom of the chapel at Hicks Mill a large and now fading collage of pictures hangs framed on the wall. There are photographs, turning brown with the years, of the cottage where he was born, of Bethel and 'Three-Eyes' at Kerley Downs and Great Deliverance chapel at Carharrack. There are other pictures, too, and a tribute to this man whose name was cherished throughout Cornwall. There is a reference to 'the hundreds and thousands he brought to Christ' and who thanked God for his life and work. In the centre is a solemn, unsmiling man, sitting in unaccustomed stillness, with a dark suit, a preacher's little white bow, a slight grizzle of hair round his balding head. You look at it and ask, was this the man who leaped and danced for joy? The picture is too serious and restrained to be credible, and as you turn from it you seem to hear the noisy surge of prayer and praise from the chapel beyond, and in the midst of all the confusion, one voice raised high above it all.

That voice shouts one word, his own reiterated battlecry and call of triumph. It takes the listener back in imagination to the quiet room of the cottage at Twelveheads where he died. It was the last word he spoke before he went 'home'. Stripped down to no more than bone covered with aged and browned skin, the old man moved a little and opened his dark eyes. He was not looking at those round his bed but far beyond, and for a moment his voice was strong again as he cried out.

'Glory!'

Recent Hodder Christian Paperbacks

The story of the heroic faith of nine Elim missionaries and their four children whose lives were taken in Rhodesia.

Phyllis Thompson

The Rainbow or the Thunder

'Their only aim was to serve the African community, to help educate them and to tell them of Jesus,' a mission spokesman told the newspaper correspondents who gathered to record the worst killing of whites since the bush war began six years earlier.

On June 23rd, 1978, the mutilated bodies, including a three-week-old baby, were found lying on the edge of a cricket pitch at the Emmanuel Secondary School, Vumba, a lonely out-post in Rhodesia's Eastern Highlands, three miles from the Mozambique border. The missionaries and their families were all from the Elim Pentecostal Church, which has its international headquarters in Cheltenham, England.

Three men, six women and four children were bayonetted or clubbed to death. The children were under seven. Before the slaughter, six of the terrorists forced the mission's 250 black children to stand together.

Less than a year before, the school had been moved 70 miles to the south to Vumba. With increasing danger from terrorists, arrangements had been finalised to move the white staff's living quarters that same week to a location ten miles away, from which they would commute.

What keeps missionaries at their post despite the evident danger? Having herself been a missionary, Phyllis Thompson asks the question with understanding and sympathy, as she uncovers a story of commitment and dedication reminiscent of the book of *Acts*.

Myrna Grant
Journey

The story of Rose Warmer: courage, faith and drama to rank with *The Hiding Place*.

Rose Warmer was a beautiful Hungarian Jewess. A student of dance and sculpture, she became a leading figure in pre-war artistic and intellectual life in Budapest. When she married against the wishes of her family, her husband enticed her into dealings with the occult and she became a medium.

In 1939 her father died. In her grief, constantly besieged by spirit voices, she turned to the Bible, finally finding Christ through a small mission hall. Embracing her new faith fervently she became a missionary to the Jews, seeking remote fearful communities cowering before Hitler's 'final solution' to the 'Jewish problem'.

As more Jews were rounded up Rose became convinced that she could not continue to hide: 'I wanted to be with them. If they were to be starved, I wanted to starve. If they were being taken over the border to be killed, I wanted to be killed with them. I felt I belonged to them.'

So began a long, agonised journey from one concentration camp to another. Again and again she escaped extermination by the barest chance. She was rejected as a renegade by those she sought to reach. In her weakened state she laboured under the whips and gun butts of the SS guards. As the war ended, she was on her way to Buchenwald to die.

Today she continues her mission work wherever there are Jews. 'Hitler has not prevailed. I am living proof that God remains faithful to His people.'

Dorothy Clarke Wilson
Twelve Who Cared

By the author of *Ten Fingers for God* and *Granny Brand*.

This is an adventure of a noted Christian writer, a rarely glimpsed view of the author and the people whose lives she has recounted. Here is the story behind the stories of her subjects – the qualities of character which drew her to them, how they impressed her and changed her life.

The reader can meet, with the author, Granny Brand and her son Dr Paul Brand, pioneer surgeon for the rehabilitation of lepers; Susette La Flesche, American Indian princess; Dorothea Dix, social reformer; Hilary Pole, brave victim of *myasthenia gravis*; Doc Prithiam, an authentic country doctor, and the other courageous Christians whose lives became legends in Dorothy Clarke Wilson's books.

Dorothy Clarke Wilson, the daughter of a Baptist preacher and wife of a Methodist Minister, has written eleven biographies, six novels, seventy religious plays and two books for children. Her books have been published in Europe, America, Scandinavia and Asia.